Your children are watching you...
what do they see?

Despite the myriad influences your children are exposed to: school ... peers ... TV ... even church attendance and activities, they will learn most of their values and attitudes about life right at home—from you. From infancy to the teen years, you are being watched and imitated. An awesome concept? Yes, but don't be discouraged; it's all part of God's perfect plan for parenting.

In the pages of *Making God Real to Your Children*, you'll discover a number of ways in which God equips you for the challenge and responsibility of being the best spiritual role model you can be for your children. By offering questions for reflection, a survey for understanding your child, fun recipes, creative craft and gift ideas, and proven methods based on the "parents' primary instruction Manual," the Bible, Sally Chall serves up plenty of satisfying food for thought. She addresses a variety of topics, ranging from praying for your child before he or she is born to fostering an excitement about knowing and worshipping God, to handling the tough issues you face as your children grow older.

Whether you're raising a preschooler or a preteen... are married, a single parent, or the only Christian parent ... you'll find helpful, encouraging, reliable advice for modeling God's love to your children. By following the counsel shared here, you can be sure that you're doing your best to make God a special part of your family's life. The rest is up to Him.

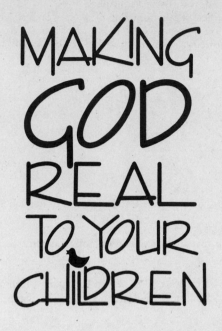

MAKING GOD REAL TO YOUR CHILDREN

SALLY LEMAN CHALL

Fleming H. Revell Company
Tarrytown, New York

Library of Congress Cataloging-in-Publication Data

Chall, Sally Leman.
    Making God real to your children / Sally Leman Chall.
        p.   cm.
    ISBN 0-8007-5407-7
    1. Family—Religious   life.   2.   Parenting—Religious   aspects—Christianity.   3. Children—Religious life. I. Title.
    BV4526.2.C38   1991
    248.8'45—dc20   91-14359
                                                                                    CIP

Copyright © 1991 by Sally Leman Chall
Published by the Fleming H. Revell Company
Tarrytown, New York 10591
Printed in the United States of America

Acknowledgments

Thank you to Christine Willet Greenwald for her enthusiasm and invaluable assistance in preparing this manuscript.

Special thanks to my brother, Dr. Kevin Leman, not only for taking the time to write the foreword for my book but also for his never-ending support and encouragement.

To Janet Anderson and my daughter Karin Chall Crimmins, thanks for the many hours of typing. I marvel at your patience in trying to decipher my margin notes and directional arrows. The manuscripts looked great.

Last but not least, to you, Wes, the Christian husband and father God knew we needed, thanks for your love and strength.

Contents

Foreword

Let me tell you right up front that I think this is a wonderful book—one that is going to be an extremely valuable help to Christian parents of children of all ages. What's more, I would feel that way about it even if the author weren't my sister. If you detect a bit of brotherly pride in those words, that's all right, too, because I am extremely proud of what Sally has done in preparing this excellent resource for Christian parents.

I'll have to admit that a little bit of the pride I feel may be coming from the fact that I feel I helped her so much with the writing of the book. Did I give her advice on how to organize it? No. Did I go over it with the proverbial fine-tooth comb and suggest changes in phrasing here and there? No, I didn't do that either. Did I spend hours on the phone giving her the benefit of my years of experience as a practicing psychologist? Wrong again.

"Well, then," somebody asks, "how exactly *did* you help her?" By being her little brother, that's how. And I have to think the experiences that came with that particular stroke of fate gave her as much material (or nearly as much, anyway) as those that came with the process of rearing three children of her own. For example, I will never forget one of those cherished times of childhood—standing over her while she slept, dangling the biggest, fattest, juiciest night crawler a little boy could find, in her face. I will always remember fondly the look of absolute horror that came across her sixteen-year-old face the instant she opened her eyes; horror that was quickly replaced by annoyance and contempt for me.

"Mother, get him out of here!"

How often I heard those words when I was a child.

I have to admit it, as a little brother I was a pretty big pain in the neck. Often her boyfriends paid me money to get lost! Nevertheless, I turned out okay, and I'm sure a large part of that was due to Sally's loving patience (despite the worm incident). On more than one occasion, she took the time to sit and patiently talk with me about things that were on my mind—giving advice when I needed it, listening when I just needed someone to talk to, and allowing me to benefit from her years of experience. (Not that she's *that much* older than I am!) And she did all that despite the fact that she wouldn't get much in return—with the exception of an occasional creepy-crawler being dangled in her face.

I ought to mention, too, that Sally's three children, Karin, Kristine, and Tom, have grown into very fine adults . . . the sort of kids any parent would be happy to claim. I expected as much because they were always neat kids, again due in large part to the guidance and nurturing Sally and her husband, Wes, gave them.

If you have read some of my books (and if you haven't, run out to your nearest store and buy several of them right now), you know I talk about Sally quite a bit. That's because she has had a profound effect on me, and although I don't tell her enough to her face, her presence in my life has been stabilizing, calming, and always an influence for good. (After all, I hardly ever dangle night crawlers in the faces of my wife and daughters!)

There is plenty of practical advice in *Making God Real to Your Children* that comes from experience, but beyond that, my sister is a scholar who knows what she is talking about. She is a student of the Bible who has been a Christian for most of her life. She knows her Bible, and she also knows the truthfulness and validity of the precepts and promises it contains. She is also a student of family-oriented journals and books, and she has distilled and refined what she has learned there to produce a book that is uniquely her own. Sally knows and understands children. She not only serves as the director of one of North America's finest preschools but she also surrounds herself daily in her classroom with sixteen little ankle-biters. Sally brings a wealth of practical experience to the reader based on her thirty plus years as a classroom teacher and mother.

Another thing that makes this book beneficial is that it is so beautifully organized. But then, I wouldn't have expected anything less from a firstborn like Sally!

As the father of four children, as a Christian, and as a psychologist with more years of experience than I would care to admit, I know that *Making God Real to Your Children* is a most timely and welcome addition to my resources. In my travels and in my private practice I often come face-to-face with Christian parents who want to know what they did wrong that made their children rebel against them and against God. Parenting has never been an easy job, and it isn't getting easier as we move further into the nineties.

That is why I am particularly happy to see Sally's book coming out at this time. I really believe that parents who read what she has to say and put her principles into practice are not likely to be asking, "Where did we go wrong?" a few years down the road.

Now bear with me for another moment or two while I do a bit of bragging about my sister.

It is not always easy to present practical, workable advice in a way that is readable and easy to digest, but Sally has done it. She has included numerous anecdotes that you will relate to and learn from. She has included questions that will guide you as you read. She gives some top priorities for Christian parents. She talks about the importance of Christian parents facing up to and admitting their own imperfections (I particularly appreciated what she had to say about this). And she gives ideas for things to do with children, games to play with them, and conversations that will give them an understanding of God's presence in their lives.

As I said earlier, I believe you are really going to enjoy this book . . . and I also believe you and your children and even your grandchildren are going to benefit from it.

Way to go, Sally. You've come up with a winner! Just like a firstborn, you did it with class.

KEVIN LEMAN

MAKING GOD REAL TO YOUR CHILDREN

1

—

Making God Real to Your Children: The Christian Parent's Primary Goal

It was a perfect day—low humidity, temperature in the low seventies with the sun shining brightly—just right for attacking the yard work, which was screaming for attention. Carol Cooper decided to weed the garden, while twenty-year-old Ted and his dad, Ed, mowed the lawn, trimmed the hedges, and raked the clippings.

The afternoon slipped away, and suddenly it was time to start supper. There were only three of them at the dinner table these days. Carol worked in the kitchen, her mind slipping back to previous years when laughter had filled the room as six Coopers gathered for meals. The others were married now and living in different parts of the country. Family life was always changing, she mused silently. Nothing ever stayed the same.

Supper over, Carol busied herself putting away the dishes while Ed read the paper and Ted took phone call after phone call as the gang made plans for the evening. No more tucking the covers around Ted, turning out the lights, and knowing that all was well, Carol sighed to herself. Nowadays it seemed that by the time she and Ed were ready to head upstairs for bed, the younger generation was just walking out the door for a night on the town.

"Don't be too late, honey—and have a good time," Carol called as Ted left. She tried not to worry, but. . . . Would he be home at a decent hour so he'd be able to get up for church in the morning? Who was driving? Was he a drinker? She knew her son was usually the designated driver. He was really a good kid.

She left a light on in the kitchen, made sure the back door was unlocked, and turned off all but one lamp in the living room before going upstairs. Ten o'clock—*was* all well?

Several hours later, she awoke with a start. The clock read 2:00 A.M. Glancing into Ted's room as she padded down the hall to the bathroom, she saw that the bed looked as it had when she'd changed the sheets the previous morning. The living room lamp still glowed through the quiet darkness.

A sense of uneasiness crept over her as she crawled back into bed and pulled up the blankets to ward off the early-morning chill.

"Ted's not home yet," she whispered, needing Ed's comfort but hesitating to awaken him unnecessarily.

"I know," came the reply. "I can't sleep either."

They lay side by side in the stillness, hearing every car pass on the street below, wondering if the next one would signal Ted's arrival. Was that it? They listened anxiously for a few moments, wishing in vain to hear the familiar rumbling of the garage door, the squeak of the back screen, Ted's sneakers scrunching across the kitchen on his way to the refrigerator.

The digital clock marked their wait—2:15 A.M., 2:30, 2:45, 3:00. This wasn't like Ted. Then the telephone's ring shattered the night quiet. Groping for the receiver in the darkness, her hand trembling and her stomach churning, Carol gathered her courage to answer.

"Hello."

"Is this the Cooper residence?"

"Yes, this is Mrs. Cooper."

"This is the sheriff's office calling. There's been an accident. Your son has been injured. Please come to the emergency room at General Hospital as quickly as possible."

The impact of that awful night, now many years ago, continues to haunt the Coopers. By the time they arrived at the hospital, their son had succumbed to the severe head injury he had sustained when a drunk driver hit the car in which he was a passenger.

Besides the unending grief and the "if onlys" and "whys" that overwhelm them, Ed and Carol wonder, in private, whether Ted is with the Lord. He always went to Sunday school and church but never said much about his personal faith or commitment to Jesus Christ. *What if . . . no, don't think about it . . .* but the thoughts persist. *If only we had talked to him about the Lord more often. He was just twenty. . . . We thought we had a lifetime.*

I could tell story after story, each filled with whys and if onlys, about shortened lives, rebellion, and the consequences of unwise choices. Somehow it is so easy for life's hectic pace to dull our sense of urgency about making sure God is real to our children and that they are basing their daily decisions about friends, activities, and choices on Him and on His Word.

What Is Most Important?

If you could make a wish list, what would you desire most for each of your children?

- a sense of self-worth
- god in his or her life
- the ability to make wise choices
- a secure and happy childhood
- meaningful school experiences
- good friends
- a wonderful mate
- a satisfying career
- enough money to live "happily ever after"

That is an admirable list, but what one area would you consider the most important? The Bible indicates over and over (and we will examine many of the passages later in this book) that as Christian parents our primary goal should be to see that each child in our family loves God, accepts the salvation offered by His Son, Jesus Christ, and matures in that faith so that someday we can stand before God as complete families in our heavenly home.

We have only *now* to make God real to our children, to share with them by word and example the joy, peace, and excitement of letting Him guide, direct, and be *Lord* of their lives. A goal? Yes! Our primary goal!

Well, you say, that sounds easy enough. We'll just take them to Sunday school and church, perhaps enroll them in Christian schools, involve them in youth groups, send them off to church camps, and make sure they say their prayers before meals and at bedtime.

But it does not work that way. Our society teaches us that if we want our children to learn to swim, we need only enroll them in swimming lessons at the YMCA. If we want our children to learn to play the piano, we must find a great piano teacher. If it is early learning we are interested in, signing them up for the best preschool in town fulfills our responsibility.

But this theory falls short where the spiritual well-being of our children is concerned. The activities the church has to offer may truly enrich our children's lives, but the responsibility for teaching them about God is ours! The great commandment found in Deuteronomy 6:4–9 tells us:

> . . . Jehovah is our God, Jehovah alone. You must love him with all your heart, soul, and might. And you must think constantly about these commandments I am giving you today. You must teach them to your children and talk about them when you are at home or out for a walk; at bedtime and the first thing in the morning. Tie them on your finger, wear them on your forehead, and write them on the doorposts of your house!

In other words, we are to be so in touch with the Lord that talking with Him and about Him becomes a natural part of our day-to-day living. When we love someone, we want to talk to him or her. When we are excited about someone in our lives, we want to introduce him or her to those we love. According to this passage of Scripture, we are expected to begin and end the day talking with and about the Lord. We are to take the time to remind ourselves and our children on a daily basis of the reality of God and of the profound difference a committed personal relationship with Him can make in our lives.

In no way am I trying to minimize the importance of the influence of pastors, youth workers, Sunday school teachers, or camp counselors and directors in the lives of our children.

Let's face it—life is far from ideal, and many persons have been brought into the Kingdom of God because of the dedication and willingness of a Christian worker to share his or her faith and to become involved in the lives of others.

But God's perfect plan is for children to learn about His love for them right in their own homes. We are our children's *first* teachers, and modern science confirms what the biblical record shows over and over, whether in the wisdom literature of the Psalms and Proverbs or in the narratives of such parent-child relationships as David and Solomon (1 Kings 2:1–4, 9:3–9; 1 Chronicles 22:5–13), Rebekah and Jacob (Genesis 25:27, 28, 27:1–46, 37:3, 4), Eunice and Timothy (2 Timothy 1–5): Parents are their children's *most influential* teachers.

God intended us to be our children's first and most influential teachers. What a responsibility!

How Do We Do It, Lord? We Need Help!

The passage from Deuteronomy 6 is certainly forceful, but just *how* can we remind ourselves and our children regularly about our God and Savior, Jesus Christ? The average Christian today would think it strange to wear key Scripture verses, written on small pieces of parchment and rolled up in long, narrow strips of leather, tied to his forehead or attached to his inner arm, closest to the heart, as did the religious leaders of Jesus' day. Neither do we copy favorite Bible verses and place them beside the front door for all who enter to take, as was the custom of the Old Testament Jews.

Yet the biblical suggestion that parents "tie on their fingers" the laws and commandments of God was based on sound principle, even though the Pharisees of Jesus' time, whose very name is synonymous with hypocrisy, missed the point. Sometimes I think we *need* a piece of bright red yarn, tied in a large bow, around one finger. It would shout at us:

- Love God above all else.
- Make Him a regular part of your family life; include Him in your thoughts and plans by consulting His Word daily, together, as a family.
- Take time for casual conversations with your children that center on the Lord, using everyday incidents to point to the wonder of God's creation or to the necessity for allowing His love to flow through us to others.

We *can* choose to incorporate the use of symbols in our homes, as this passage suggests, which will call to mind God's love and care for the family. Try hanging a picture of Jesus or some other appropriate Christian artwork in a child's bedroom or in the family room, living room, or dining room, where family members and visitors can enjoy its beauty and meaning. Occasionally replacing such artwork with loans of history's great religious masterpieces available at your local library, or inexpensive prints or posters from a Christian bookstore, will stimulate good discussions and keep the reminders fresh.

Be sure to provide Bible-oriented tapes, books, and puzzles for use in the home. Saturating the minds of family members with "what is true and good and right . . . pure and lovely, and . . . fine" (Philippians 4:8) at an early age is good training in an important biblical principle and gives them a firm basis on which to make choices regarding modes of entertainment, language, and attitudes.

Carefully chosen jewelry with a Christian theme can also help a child to remember that God loves him or her. But remember: The emphasis cannot be on the symbol and its show value.

Eight-year-old Joelle looked forward to Vacation Bible School as a very special part of her summer. Before she left the house that first day, her mom handed her an old Bible to take along.

Joelle was not pleased. She had really wanted to take the Bible from the coffee table—the beautiful one her mom had given to her dad for his college graduation. Carefully dusted and placed, just so, it was an untouchable part of her home's decor. Christmastime always found it open to the account of Jesus' birth.

Joelle was embarrassed when it came time for the highlight of VBS opening exercises—the sword drill.

"Draw your swords," called Pastor Phil. One hundred kids, filled with anticipation, lifted their Bibles high in the air. All but Joelle.

Pastor Phil named the Scripture passages to search for. "John 3:16."

"John 3:16!" the kids shouted back. All but Joelle.

"Ready?" called Pastor Phil. "Charge!"

One hundred kids scrambled to find the text in hopes of being the first to stand and read it out loud. All but Joelle. She sat quietly, affecting boredom, her Bible in her lap.

"What's the matter, Joelle? Don't you want to play?" asked the pastor.

"No," Joelle replied halfheartedly. "This Bible is just an old decoration."

Joelle's mom heard about the incident later in the week. The realization that her young daughter perceived God's Word only as an ornament was dismaying. Things had to start changing if Joelle was ever going to understand that the Bible is to be read and digested so its truths saturate all of life, affecting the lives of God's children in the most practical ways. Joelle needed to know that the Bible is not just for show. It is real! And so is its Author!

Making God Real—A Few Starting Principles

If it sounds as if this book is a parenting course with a concentration on God—good! It is! Is making God real to your children a goal of utmost importance? Your primary goal? Even very young children can develop the concept of a loving, saving God as they observe their parents' godly behavior, "hear" a lifestyle based on His Word, and feel the caring that flows from parents who attempt to demonstrate God's love.

We talk a lot and read a lot in an abundance of parenting literature about the physical, intellectual, emotional, and social areas of a child's life. Yet somehow the young child's spiritual development is placed in a category all its own.

But the Bible tells us we humans are made in the image of God. We are spiritual beings, and we cannot separate the spiritual from the nonspiritual. God wants His Way to permeate all of life. How can we model it for our children?

Here are three foundational principles to remember as you read the following chapters. Use them as a basis for applying the other ideas in the book.

Principle Number One: God's Word Is Our Instruction Manual.

As Christians we can trust God's Word to serve as our primary instruction manual for parenting. No, the Bible does not specifically tell us whether or not the latest fad in kids' toys will help or harm our little ones or how to detect whether or not an adolescent is using drugs. But the Bible contains broad (and some quite detailed) guidelines for human conduct and for the development of our relationships with God and our fellow human beings—including parents and children.

We have already examined one such guideline from Deuteronomy 6, that our lives as Christians are to be so intertwined with our Father's and with Jesus Christ's, and so permeated with the power of the Holy Spirit, that teaching our children about Him and His ways is a natural part of the daily functions of our lives—in the home, outside the home, and all through the happenings of our days.

We will examine other biblical guidelines as we work through issues of parental modeling, positive and negative reinforcement, child discipline, our use of time, and how to help our children accept and walk with God.

I am reminded of 2 Timothy 3:15–17:

> . . . when you were a small child, you were taught the holy Scriptures; and it is these that make you wise to accept God's salvation by trusting in Christ Jesus. The whole Bible was given to us by inspiration from God and is useful to teach us what is true and to make us realize what is wrong in our lives; it straightens us out and helps us do what is right. It is God's way of making us well prepared at every point, fully equipped to do good to everyone.

Fully equipped. . . . I love to be in the kitchen just puttering. And it is a good thing I do, because that is where I spend 90 percent of my time when I am at home. Anyone can prepare a meal with limited tools, but a good cook with a *fully equipped* kitchen can turn out truly elegant cuisine.

Just think—the Scriptures *fully equip* us for all we face in life, and that includes Christian parenting!

We have at our disposal today countless books, seminars, and talk shows, in both the Christian and secular realms, zeroing in on the subject of parenting. Although these can be wonderfully helpful, their sheer numbers and differing opinions can be confusing. Whom can we trust? Whose advice do we implement in raising our families?

As Christian parents, we need to consider prayerfully anything we read or hear in the light of Scripture and in its relationship to our particular family situations. Each child is different; each family is unique. Principle number two can help us know how to apply God's Word to our specific needs.

Principle Number Two: Know Your Child.

One key text long claimed by Christian parents is Proverbs 22:6. The King James Version states it this way: "Train up a child in the way he should go: and when he is old, he will not depart from it."

That sounds pretty cut and dried, doesn't it? Many Christian moms and dads have assumed that if they laid down the law about how to live an upright moral life according to their understanding of biblical dos and don'ts, they could depend on this promise to mean that their children would not stray from God and the Church. Yet all around us we see people from apparently strong Christian homes who have rejected the faith their parents tried to instill in them.

For many years I have puzzled over this mystery text. All of my whys usually culminated in the assumption that no one ever knows what really goes on in another person's home. Superficial appearances may not reflect reality. We tend to parent our children according to the models we grew up with and not necessarily according to God's directions.

But let's look at this verse more carefully. The Living Bible says, "Teach a child to choose the right path, and when he is older he will remain upon it." According to the Ryrie Study Bible, the original meaning of the verse is, "Teach a child *in the way he should go*, which literally means 'according to his way' i.e., the child's habits and interests. The instruction must take into account his individuality and inclination and be in keeping with his degree of physical and mental development."

This sheds an entirely different light on the verse and provides an important parenting principle. The often-voiced concept that every child is a unique human being created by God is really true, and a foundational task in Christian parenting, and in making God real to our children, is to *know each child*.

Getting to know each of our children requires a considerable investment of time, patience, and prayer. We need to become actively involved in their lives, yet know when it is appropriate to stand back and observe. Are we ready to "listen much, speak little, and not become angry" as the Bible teaches in James 1:19, 20?

Sharing feelings and experiences with each child, coupled with sharing our hopes, fears, and perceptions with our mates, is vital as we strive together to know and encourage each child in the family.

Most couples dream of celebrating their first anniversary

enjoying dinner by candlelight at a nice restaurant. My husband and I exchanged anniversary wishes in the maternity wing of our local hospital, where several days before I had given birth to a precious little girl, Karin.

Kristine was born two years and nine months later. I remember looking down at her sweet face and thinking how truly different she was from Karin, even though she had the same parents.

Thomas came along three years later. The girls were thrilled to welcome a little brother into our family!

I knew as a young parent that our children were outwardly unique. The girls' hair coloring was different. Kris wore glasses earlier than Karin and loved the out-of-doors, including fishing. Karin was quieter than Kris in groups and wanted nothing whatsoever to do with baiting a hook! Good-natured Tom loved sports and life in general from the time he was knee-high.

It is easy to know a lot of superficial things about our children. But sometimes it is difficult to understand how and why our children *feel* and *respond* to life's everyday situations.

Yet Proverbs 22:6 tells us that it is tremendously important to grasp these subtler differences so that we can adapt our parenting techniques to each child's God-given personality and gifts. As we get to know each child *on the inside*, we will be better able to meet his or her needs and to grow together as a family.

The following pages contain one tool that may help you to know your child better. Take a few quiet moments and work through the exercise for each of your children. You may find it easier to complete for one, more difficult for another. That's all right, for you will be discovering much about your own relationship to that child in the process.

Understanding My Child

Child's name＿＿＿＿＿＿ Age＿＿＿＿＿

1. When he/she has disobeyed, does he/she respond positively to
   a. a time-out period in a special chair or separate room?
   b. a simple *no*?
   c. withdrawal of privileges?
   d. reasoning/discussion?
   e. a firm, deliberate spanking?
   f. a mild swat on the behind?
   g. a holding period in your arms?
   h. ＿＿＿＿＿＿＿＿＿＿＿＿＿＿＿＿＿＿＿＿?

2. Sensitivity: When embarrassed or uncomfortable in certain situations, does he/she show these feelings by
   a. hiding his/her head or self?
   b. blushing?
   c. aggressive actions?
   d. negative comments?
   e. pouting?
   f. withdrawal?
   g. complaining of headache/stomachache?
   h. verbalizing them?
   i. ＿＿＿＿＿＿＿＿＿＿＿＿＿＿＿＿＿＿＿＿?

3. Responsibility: Does he/she usually handle responsibility appropriate to his/her age and developmental level?*
   a. Yes.
   b. No.
   What attitude does he/she exhibit when asked to perform a task?
   a. Cheerfulness.
   b. Grumpiness.
   c. Discouragement.
   d. Anxiety.
   e. _____.
   Must things be done perfectly? Is he/she
   a. pleased with the accomplishment?
   b. seldom satisfied?
   c. finished on time?
   d. finished any old time?

4. Does he/she handle new situations
   a. by worrying?
   b. with ease?
   c. by withdrawal?

5. Is he/she usually happy and confident
   a. with new situations?
   b. meeting new people?
   c. at school?

---

* For information on age-appropriateness, the following resources may be helpful: Ralph Matteson and Thom Black, *Discovering Your Child's Design* (Elgin, Illinois: David C. Cook, 1989). Foster Cline, M.D., and Jim Fay, *Parenting With Love and Logic: Teaching Children Responsibility* (Colorado Springs, Colorado: Navpress, 1990). Marguerite Kelly and Elia Parsons, *The Mother's Almanac* (New York: Doubleday, 1975).

---

d. at church?
e. at home?
f. in other social situations?

6. What are his/her fears?

7. Relationships: In the family does he/she
   a. talk respectfully to parents?
   b. generally get along well with brothers, sisters, cousins?
   If not, is there clear evidence of
   a. jealousy?
   b. competition?
   c. dislike?
   Are these negative feelings directed toward anyone in particular?
   Outside the home does he/she
   a. make friends easily with younger children, older children, peers?
   b. maintain friendships?
   c. become easily influenced by friends?
   d. tend to be a follower—for better or worse?
   e. tend to be a leader—for better or worse?
   f. exhibit normal or excessive loyalty toward his/her friends?
   g. relate well to teachers, employers, pastors, coaches?
   Does the telephone ring for him/her
   a. seldom?
   b. often?
   How often is he/she invited to a friend's house?

8. List his/her abilities, interests_____

   _____.

9. What does he/she want to be when a grown-up?
10. What does he/she think are the important things in life?*

Once we start to understand each of our children on the inside, several factors become operative.

1. We are able to encourage each child to pursue interests, hobbies, school activities, studies, and relationships that are suitable to his/her personality. The key word is suitable— what was suitable for our Tom may not have been suitable for Karin or Kris. *Knowing the child* helps us as parents to give wise guidance and to avoid the stereotyping and generalizing that damage so many sensitive children.

2. We can apply scriptural principles to our children's needs on a more individual basis. Again, as we seek God daily in our own lives, He can give us wisdom to know how His Word applies to our children's problems and joys as well. And He can help us to know how to share scriptural insights at times and in ways that will appeal to our children.

3. We can pray specifically for each child's needs. God will give us wisdom in how to pray, perhaps through His Word, perhaps through the encouragement and/or insight of Christian friends who are experiencing or have experienced children with similar needs and gifts.

But what about those times when our prayers seem to bounce off the ceiling? Even then, the Scriptures tell us, God will help us if we ask Him to. Romans 8:26–28 says:

---

* Another excellent resource to help you know your child is *Discover Your Child's Gifts* by Don and Katie Fortune, Chosen Books, 1989.

. . . by our faith—the Holy Spirit helps us with our daily problems and in our praying. For we don't even know what we should pray for, nor how to pray as we should; but the Holy Spirit prays for us with such feeling that it cannot be expressed in words. And the Father who knows all hearts knows, of course, what the Spirit is saying as he pleads for us in harmony with God's own will. And we know that all that happens . . . is working for our good if we love God and are fitting into His plans.

I am convinced, from personal experience, that the God who never ran out of ideas or power when He created the universe, the God who is Himself a Father, can give us the ideas and strength we need to parent our children creatively and individually.

Principle Number Three: Don't Drive a Great Idea Into the Ground!

Often in my reading over the years I have run across a parenting gem that sounded terrific. "Wow," I've exclaimed to myself. "Why didn't I think of that when . . . ?"

If you find this happening to you, watch out! Bombarding children with even a great concept can backfire!

A case in point: A few years ago, when my brother Kevin Leman wrote his first book, *Parenthood Without Hassles* (*Well, Almost*) (Harvest House, 1979) he advised moms and dads:

We need to be providing decision-making opportunities for our children so that they have a broad, rich environment in which to make decisions that affect their lives. Then someday they will be able to make the kind of momentous decisions that adult life requires of them.

The whole idea of giving children choices and making them accountable for their actions was new to many of us. A long-time friend of mine could hardly wait to try these practical ideas on her youngest child. And try she did, over and over again, until one day he exclaimed, "That book again?"

Remember, moderation is a key consideration in implementing any new approach. We need to use common sense when we deal with our children. Develop an awareness (partially gained through trial and error) about when to back off. Ask God for His guidance, and be sensitive to receiving and acting on it.

The Time to Begin Is Now

If making God real to our children is our primary goal, we can't begin soon enough! Blessed is the child whose mother and father began before birth to prepare their hearts and minds for Christian parenthood and who started communicating the love of God through Jesus from birth-day on.

But blessed, too, is the child whose parents take hold of their responsibility to make God real at *any* stage in the child-raising process. You may feel a bit awkward at first, as I did, about making more obvious, active mention and implementation of your faith in your family's life, but teaching a child about God is tremendously exciting and worth enduring any initial unease.

We are ready now to explore more specific ways in which we can make God real to our children.

Questions for Thought

1. In what specific ways can I apply Deuteronomy 6:4–9 to help me model God's love in my home?

2. Complete the questionnaire "Understanding My Child" for each of your children, then reread items 1, 2, and 3 on page 29. What action can I take to help my child with (her shyness, his need for friends, her perfectionism, and so on)?

3. How do I feel when I try to talk with my children about God?

4. Where do I most sense my need for God's help in making Him real to my children right now?

2

Big Brother and Little Sister Are Watching You (Or, What They See Is What You Get)

Have you ever called a friend on the telephone and jumped right into a conversation, only to find that you are talking to her daughter?

"I'm sorry, Holly," you exclaim, "but you sounded just like your mother."

Or perhaps you are listening to the church choir sing the anthem some Sunday morning when a friend in the row behind you leans over to say, "Your son Johnny looks just like your husband when he sings." You look up at Johnny in the choir loft and, yes, he *does* hold his head like Ron.

Children are great imitators, and they learn by watching the adults around them. That's us, Mom and Dad! Our children walk, talk, and laugh the way we do. We may even see ourselves in their facial expressions.

But more important, our offspring learn most of their values and attitudes about life and eternity by example—*our* example. If God is going to become real to our children, we each need to take an inventory of the priorities and attitudes

---

we are exhibiting in our day-to-day lives. Do they match up to God's standards as revealed to us in the Bible? Whether they do or don't, our children's lives will be affected dramatically. We are being watched!

In the next few pages, let's examine what I see as the top three priorities for the Christian who has one or more children and how maintaining or ignoring these priorities affects the little imitators who are watching us. Don't be discouraged if some areas of your life need work. Jesus promised deep inner joy to those of us who *hunger and thirst* after His kind of righteousness—and He promised to satisfy those appetites! (*See* Matthew 5:6 KJV.) If we are lacking in some of the following categories, He can give us the wisdom and understanding we need to fill that void.

God or the World—Who Gets Top Billing?

The number-one priority for the Christian parent is his or her personal relationship to God. Ask yourself:

- Have I recognized my need of a Savior?
- Have I invited Jesus Christ to be that Savior, asking His forgiveness for my sin of rebellion against Him?
- Do I continue to ask Him to cleanse me from sin on a daily basis?
- Is God so real to me that I talk to Him naturally throughout the day and spend time listening as He talks to me through His Word, through my pastor, through Christian teachers and friends?

It is impossible to give away something we do not possess. It is impossible to make God real to our children if He is not real to us. Yes, we can provide Christian religious training for our children, but they need to see Christianity as our relationship with the living God through His Son, Jesus Christ. They need to see us allow that relationship to chart the direction of our lives. Otherwise, religious training may serve only to point out our hypocrisy and double standards.

If this concept of a living relationship with God through Jesus sounds confusing, ask God to reveal Himself to you. Get into His holy Word, the Bible. Within its pages, His Holy Spirit will not only reveal your need but also provide God's answer—His Son. Find a modern translation of the Scriptures such as the New International Version (International Bible Society), which is excellent for study. *The Living Bible* is a paraphrased edition that reads like a novel, is easily understood, and makes Bible reading exciting. I like to use them together. Devotional books and commentaries can help you to understand the Scriptures better, but don't substitute them for the Bible itself.

If finding time to read is difficult, or if you are not a reader, cassette tapes of the Scriptures are available. Play them at home or on the way to work. Christian music, especially hymns and songs with Scripture lyrics, can also feed God's Word into your mind and heart as you drive or work around the house.

It is also tremendously important for you to find a church where God's Word is preached. True, Christians can grow in their faith under the isolated conditions of a prisoner-of-war camp or a totalitarian regime, but that is not God's ideal plan. God designed Christians to grow best in fellowship with each other under the teaching of a godly pastor. Look around until you find a church home where you sense the presence of God and a loving, Christian atmosphere.

If you already have a relationship with Jesus Christ, you are aware, at least theoretically, that it needs to take first priority in your life. God spelled that out way back when He gave Moses the Ten Commandments:

> You shall have no other gods before me. You shall not make for yourself an idol in the form of anything in heaven above or on the earth beneath or the waters below . . . for I . . . am a jealous God, punishing the children for the sin of the fathers to the third and fourth generation of those who hate me, but showing love to a thousand generations of those who love me and keep my commandments.
>
> Exodus 20:3–6 NIV

God obviously wants to be first in our lives! Not just in our lip service or on Sunday mornings, but in a way that ensures that He comes before anything else on earth in our affections and loyalties.

If making Him first in our lives is so important to God, how crucial it is that we model that priority before our children! How can we do it effectively?

By Developing Regular and Consistent Devotional and Prayer Times.

For some this may mean significant time spent with the Lord and in His Word each morning or evening. For others, larger amounts of time set aside two or three days a week coupled with a brief devotional reading every day may be more meaningful and realistic. The important words are *regularity* and *consistency*.

Why? Both for our own sakes and for our children's. Moms and dads who are refreshed and fed by God's Word and by time spent asking for and receiving His wisdom make better parents. Knowing that Mom and Dad are consulting God and His Word about everyday joys and problems provides our children with tremendous security and a dynamic model.

By Welcoming Our Children to Our Quiet Times Naturally and Lovingly.

"But my kids always interrupt me when I'm trying to read the Bible. After a while I just give up."

Interruptions? No! Our children's natural desire to see what we are doing and to be with us often provides God-ordained teaching moments, and this is one of them. How wonderful for them to see us delving into His Word! So don't spoil a chance to share His love by getting frustrated. Try saying something like this:

"Mommy is reading God's Word right now. Would you like to sit on my lap and read along? No? That's fine—you play quietly for a few minutes and then we'll make a game out of cleaning up the living room before we go to visit Grandma."

You may have to be lovingly firm a few times, but if you are, your children will sense the importance of your time with God. As they grow older, develop more regular sleeping habits and, eventually, enter school, you will have many opportunities to give the Bible your undivided attention. In the meantime, even small portions of God's Word, regularly ingested through Bible reading or through listening to Scripture and music cassettes, will be used by the Holy Spirit in your life.

By Making Regular Corporate Worship With the People of God and Regular Times of Christian Education "Givens" in Our Family Schedules.

Children who grow up knowing that church and Sunday school are (a) nonnegotiable items on the family agenda and (b) important enough to Mom and Dad so that *they* go, too, are much more likely to continue church and Sunday school attendance in adulthood. Studies show that sending the kids to Sunday school but not accompanying them conveys a strong message to children: "This is not *really* important to my parents."

By Letting God's Word Be the Strongest Influence on Our Everyday Behavior Toward Our Family Members, Neighbors, Friends, and Strangers.

We will deal with some concrete examples a bit later, but if the truths we gain in our devotional lives and on Sunday morning are not lived out in the practical issues of life, our children will sense our hypocrisy long before we do.

And a Little Child Shall Lead Them. . . .

Before we move on to the Christian parent's second priority, one reminder. Jesus told us that unless we are converted *and* become as little children, we will not see the Kingdom of God (Matthew 18:3). Jesus was not telling us to be childish but childlike. Let's check to see if we exhibit the following childlike qualities in our faith:

Activity. Little ones are busy from the time they get up in the morning until they are put to bed at night—and even then, some want to keep going. Are we active and full of energy as we serve the Lord?

Need for rest. When children become overtired, they get cranky and impossible to deal with. Are we resting in the Lord through prayer and times of quiet meditation?

Need for exercise. A child's busy little body requires exercise for growth. Do we as Christian parents exercise our spiritual muscles through private and corporate worship, fellowship, prayer, and the study of God's Word?

Imitation. Children are great imitators! Do we imitate our Heavenly Father? Can others—especially our families—see Christ in the way we live?

Dependency. How our children need us! Are we as dependent on God for our every need as our children are on us? Are our children aware of our thankfulness for His care?

Trust. Picture a two-year-old free-falling into his father's welcoming arms after being tossed toward the ceiling. He shows no fear, only the convulsive laughter of a little one who trusts his dad completely. Do we trust God for our salvation and the welfare of the family? No matter what comes along in life, do we trust Him to be right there with us? Do we believe what is written in His holy Word? Little children believe what their parents tell them.

Curiosity. We all know that little children get into everything and ask a million questions. They are always touching, tasting, smelling, seeing, and listening as they explore the world around them. Are we curious about God's Word? Do we allow its contents to help us understand our world? Are we teachable?

Enthusiasm. Little ones are easily excited about almost anything—from a beautiful butterfly to lunch at McDonald's. Are we enthusiastic about our faith? Does it show?

Eagerness to please. Young children like to please the adults in their lives. We may not always believe that, but just try showing your pleasure in a picture your daughter has created or in your son's attempt to set the table. You will see smiles galore!

Do we try to please the God who loves us?

Hunger.   Newborns are always hungry—or so it seems to Mom and Dad at 3:00 A.M. For the first few months, baby's entire diet is milk. Gradually fruits and vegetables are added, until that tiny digestive tract matures enough to handle meats on a daily basis.

Are we feeding constantly on God's Word? Are we growing by leaps and bounds? Are we able to dig in and enjoy spiritual meat, or are we anemic for lack of a proper diet?

Honesty.   The Easter holiday was drawing near, and Mrs. Bingham thought her preschool class would enjoy playing a musical listening game where bunnies run and jump in the fields. The children were to jump into their holes (colored rings on the floor) at the sound of a drum; at the sound of a bell, they were to stand still.

Thinking she should demonstrate, Mrs. Bingham (hands atop her head for ears) jumped in and out of the colored rings. The children watched patiently.

"Did I look like a bunny?" Mrs. Bingham asked breathlessly when the song ended.

"More like a big rabbit!" said little Mandy.

Are we honest with God?

The importance of priority number one—the Christian parent's relationship with God—will be a recurring theme throughout the rest of this book. To repeat: *We cannot make God real to our children if He is not real to us first!*

Peace or War—What Do Our Children See?

Priority number two: *Christian parents need to place their marriage relationships second only to their personal relationships with Jesus Christ!* Do our children see their parents living in mutually loving and helping relationships, or is the family front a war zone? Fortunate, indeed, is the child whose mother and father respect and love each other. A harmonious marriage relationship provides priceless security and stability on which a child can build his or her life. It also provides a model that can influence future generations positively.

Perhaps you have attended a wedding recently, as I have, in which the couple has included a reading or musical rendition of 1 Corinthians 13, commonly referred to as the "love chapter." What a great chance for a personal checkup! Note especially verses four and five:

> Love is very patient and kind, never jealous or envious, never boastful or proud, never haughty or selfish or rude. Love does not demand its own way. It is not irritable or touchy. It does not hold grudges and will hardly even notice when others do it wrong.

The chapter goes on to say that when one person loves another, he or she will be loyal, believe in and defend him, and always expect the best.

Is that what our children see in our relationships with our mates? On a situation-by-situation, moment-by-moment basis? Most of us, if asked, would say, "Of course I respect my husband/wife. Of course I love him/her." And, given the overall picture, we really think that is what we are portraying to our children.

But children focus on the little things. Does Dad make a

big deal when Mom can't find the car keys in her purse or when the mashed potatoes are lumpy? Does Mom belittle Dad, even teasingly, about his lack of handyman skills or the time it takes him to accomplish household tasks? Is either parent domineering of the other, offering frequent directives and sighing with exasperation when demands are not met?

Children understand best what they have experienced. If they see 1 Corinthians 13 love between their parents, they will know Mom and Dad are really trying to walk Jesus' way in the nitty-gritty stuff of life. And they will understand God's love better and grow up to pass it on to their mates and children. If they see selfishness, impatience, rudeness, and put-downs—guess what they will think of our efforts to make God real, and guess what their mates and children will have to live with someday?

We parents need to make our second, highly important priority—the marriage relationship—a visible one for our children to observe with delight! We need to take time for each other on a daily basis, with affectionate touches and caring words. (Some psychologists say we need seven hugs a day for good emotional and mental health!) We need to take time for regular dates, even if it is only a nightly walk, a trip to the corner coffee shop for dessert, or a brief rendezvous downtown for lunch.

In his *Six-Point Plan for Raising Happy, Healthy Children* (Andrews and McMeel, 1989), author, psychologist, and nationally syndicated columnist John Rosemond tells of friends who used to give their children their undivided attention from the moment everyone arrived home at the end of the day. In return, however, the parents noticed an increase in disobedience, crankiness, and childish demands. Says Rosemond, "The kids had taken over!"

So the parents decided on a new plan of action: For the first half hour after everyone came home, the children had to play in their own rooms or outside, while Mom and Dad had some adult talk and fixed dinner. Rosemond suggests that in so doing, the parents "moved their marriage back to center stage." The surprising result was better-behaved, polite, independent children—who were secure in their parents' love!

Don't be afraid to take time for your marriage!

If your marriage suffers from deeper communicative, sexual, or financial difficulties, *don't hesitate* to study God's Word, read some of the many Christian self-help books on the market, and/or seek counseling from a minister or other recommended professional. You owe it to God, to yourselves, and to your children to root out the problems and get your marriage on the kind of solid foundation that will enable healthy physical, mental, emotional, and spiritual growth in your home.

But I'm a Single Parent. . . .

It would be understandably tempting at this point for the single parents among us, or those parents whose mates are not Christians, to be very discouraged.

"We're not a 'traditional' family; perhaps we never will be! How can I model God's concept of a secure Christian home without a mate, or with a mate who refuses to honor God and His Word?"

First, remember that God promises:

> For your Maker is your husband, the Lord of hosts is His name; And your Redeemer is the Holy One of Israel. . . . For the Lord has called you Like a woman forsaken and grieved in spirit, Like a youthful wife when you were refused. . . . All your children shall be

taught by the Lord, And great shall be the peace of
your children.

Isaiah 54:5, 6, 13 NKJV

Even in the most secure of Christian marriages, there are
times of loneliness when only God's love and the presence of
the Holy Spirit can offer comfort. How much more does God
offer His enfolding love, companionship, and help to the single parent, or to one whose spouse is spiritually cold?

Whether you are widowed, divorced, separated, or never
wed, Christ's redeeming love offers a fresh start and the security of His everlasting arms to cradle your children.

Here are a few areas in which you may need to seek His
wisdom, direction, and creative ideas:

1. Uncles and aunts, grandparents, and friends at church
can provide opportunities for your children to interact with
missing role models of the opposite sex. More adults and
children are becoming sensitive to this need. Ask God to
guide your intuition in choosing good role models for your
youngsters, and then don't hesitate to request their help.

2. If you have hang-ups with the opposite sex as a result of
previous experiences, see your pastor or ask him or her to
refer you to a counselor. For your children's sakes, as well as
your own, do your best to resolve such difficulties with God's
help.

3. Choose opposite-sex friends only with God's direction.

These are only a few very simple suggestions. Many fine
Christian books are available to help you deal, in detail, with

the particular needs of the single Christian parent.* Take advantage of them.

"Dad and Mom Don't Care About Me!"

We have talked about priorities number one and two—our personal relationship with Jesus Christ and our marriage relationships. Now we come to priority number three, a cardinal tenet of Christian parenting: *Our children need to know down deep, by our actions and our words, that they, their activities, their joys and hurts are vitally important to us.*

Bob was a terrific guy, with a smile and a handshake for everyone. He was always fixing something for someone, always willing to lend a helping hand, always busy on committees at church.

But if someone in Bob's family needed something, forget it! He was too busy or too tired. How long did it take his children to figure out who was really important? Not long. As an adult, his son continues to be bitter and continually struggles with his feelings toward a dad who, quite frankly, failed his son.

Do our children see God in us? Does His unconditional love for each of us—that love we bask in day after day as we get to know Him better—shine through to our little ones?

A young child's idea of who God is can be an extension of how he or she sees the people around him or her—especially parents, grandparents, Christian workers, and teachers. It is a humbling experience to realize the example we are setting for all children with whom we come in contact but especially for

---

* The following books may be helpful: Robert Barnes, *Single Parenting: A Wilderness Journey* (Wheaton, Illinois: Tyndale House Publishers, 1984). Robert Barnes, *Single Parents Survival Guide* (Wheaton, Illinois: Tyndale House Publishers, 1987). Larry Burkett, *Complete Financial Guide for Single Parents* (Wheaton, Illinois: Victor Books, 1991).

our own children. We can never measure up to God, but He can be our model.

The following chart describes some of God's characteristics and suggests how we parents can translate them to our children by our parenting behavior.

GOD IS . . .

JUST AND FAIR
He gives us free will to choose and holds us accountable for our decisions and actions.

LOVING
He offers unconditional love. He loved the world, giving His only Son.

UNCHANGING
He is the same yesterday, today, and forever.

THE ULTIMATE AUTHORITY
In heaven and on earth.

KIND AND MERCIFUL
To all—even the ungrateful and wicked. We are saved by grace through no merit of our own.

THE GODLY PARENT . . .

Listens before deciding. Administers loving discipline using principles of logical consequences for our behavior.

Loves each child for the person he or she is, not for the person the parent wishes him or her to be.

Demonstrates consistent behavior. Says what he or she means and follows through.

Believes parental authority is God-given. Strives for balance between permissiveness and dictatorship.

Offers verbal and nonverbal responses that convey kindness, respect, and love.

FORGIVING
Removes our sin and remembers it no more.

Never holds grudges. Does not bring up the past.

LISTENING
Hears us when we pray, giving His undivided attention.

Listens with interest and without condemnation before taking action.

PATIENT
Slow to anger.

Listens first, then asks questions. Never disciplines when angry.

DESIRES RELATIONSHIP WITH HIS CHILDREN
Wants what is best for us. Has given us the Bible, the Holy Spirit, and prayer so we can know Him.

Works to build a close-knit family unit where individuals respect one another. Wants what is best for the child.

PROVIDER
Supplies all of our needs.

Desires to meet the needs of the child materially, physically, emotionally, spiritually, and intellectually.

COMFORTER
Through the work of the Holy Spirit.

Gives comfort to children as need arises.

ALL-POWERFUL
We can be secure knowing He is in control.

Is a source of strength and security for the child.

HELPER
He is our help in time of trouble.

Is ready to help when necessary.

ALL-KNOWING
Knew us before we were born. Even the hairs of our heads are numbered.

Strives to know and understand each child.

OUR FRIEND
Closer than a brother. Will never leave or forsake us. Is first our Creator, Savior, Lord.

Is a parent first; friendship comes later as relationship matures.

WISE
Knows what is best for us; doesn't always give us what we want.

Frequently does know what is best for the child. If in doubt, asks God's guidance, consults other authorities. Allows choices based on child's maturity level.

Our children are watching us. What do they see?

We have discussed the three top priorities for Christian parents. Now let's look at four crucial areas in which our children regularly observe whether or not we are exercising those priorities.

Consistency

Sunday mornings are extra busy for churchgoing families, and the minister's family is no exception. One morning after church Jason hopped into the car, where his mom, brother, and pastor dad were waiting to head home. Kids will be kids, and by the time the family turned into the parsonage driveway, a tired mom was yelling and screaming (or so it seemed to Jason). In the chaos that followed, the boys were sent to their room.

While they changed their clothes, Jason sighed, "I wish Mom would be as nice to us as she is to the people at church." As the words tumbled from his lips, he caught a glimpse of his mother standing in the bedroom doorway. Nothing more was ever said—nor did it need to be.

Do our kids feel that way about us? Are we different people at home than we are at work, at church, or with our friends? Do we treat our family members with the same evenhandedness and consideration we treat others with? Or do our family members feel like second-class citizens?

Each family member is priceless, and time passes so quickly. The little boy you tuck into his first big bed will overlap both ends before you know it. We need to show our respect for and enjoyment of one another in our consistent, courteous behavior. There is much wise counsel in the old saying, "Treat your family like friends and your friends like family." Our children are watching us. What do they see?

Family Ties

"We don't see very much of my parents," said Cindy, the mother of two small children. Her matter-of-fact manner made me realize how lucky my husband and I are to enjoy super relationships with our children and their families.

"We just can't stand being with our parents. There's always trouble," said Tim, as his wife, Jill, nodded in agreement. "If we don't do things just their way, they pile on the guilt. You wouldn't believe what we go through every time we're together."

This young couple, the parents of four small children, seemed determined to maintain the status quo no matter how much members of their Bible study group encouraged them to do otherwise. Mending fences with Mom and Dad was not a priority item at that point in their lives.

Many families spend the best years of their lives "a feudin' and a fightin' and a fussin'," as the old song goes, or completely ignoring one another. Some make up before it is too late, but far too many others shed tears over opportunities for reconciliation that are lost forever.

How sad for everyone concerned! Unity in the immediate family is terribly important, but enjoying the extended family (grandparents, aunts, uncles, and cousins) is important as well. Regardless of how hard we try to conceal behind bedroom doors our dismay over Aunt Susie's irritability or Grandpa's domineering manner, our feelings will eventually be conveyed to our children. Yes, family relational problems can be complex, but we have a big God who delights in solving problems and who offers guidelines for those solutions in His Word:

> Blessed are the peacemakers, for they will be called sons of God.
>
> Matthew 5:9 NIV

> Stop being mean, bad-tempered and angry. Quarreling, harsh words, and dislike of others should have no place in your lives. Instead, be kind to each other, tenderhearted, forgiving one another, just as God has forgiven you because you belong to Christ.
>
> Ephesians 4:31, 32

Even if Aunt Susie and Grandpa are not willing to change, God can help us with *our* attitudes. And just as our children pick up on family tensions, they will realize when Mom and Dad are making genuine efforts to be peacemakers.

Fortunate are the children who see Mom and Dad speaking with love and respect to *their* parents, who see relatives included in family activities in a natural, loving way, and who are taught to show their love for extended family members near and far on a regular basis.

Wealthy are the children who can spend the night at Grandma and Grandpa's baking cookies together and curling up on a grandparent's lap to hear a favorite story. What warm memories are created by overnights spent with uncles, aunts, and cousins.

From the time our Tom was three years old, Grandpa Chall came for him in the lumber company pickup truck at nine o'clock sharp on Saturday mornings for their weekly "coffee" with several other businessmen in downtown Jamestown, New York. Grape juice, doughnuts, eggs, bacon, and even a small birthday cake complete with candles on March 10 made those Saturdays special. But the most fun of all was being one of the guys. Tom really felt grown-up when his dad gave him money to buy the morning treat. Even during those teen years when it was in style to sleep in, Tom rarely missed a Saturday. At twenty-four, he was still meeting his eighty-two-year-old grandpa for breakfasts. We think it is quite a memory. Tom does, too.

If we make honest attempts to love our extended family members unconditionally as God loves us, perhaps our children will catch a glimpse of what God is like in us. The Bible says that if Christ is our personal Savior, our bodies become the temples of His Spirit. Our children are watching. What do they see?

What Happens When We're Old and Gray?

Remember the old saying, "Charity begins at home"? Perhaps that piece of folk wisdom actually came from 1 Timothy 5:4, which teaches that the responsibility for the care of needy parents rests squarely on the shoulders of children and grandchildren. The verse doesn't specify "the oldest in the family" or "the daughter in the family." Nor does it indicate that such care is the son's financial responsibility. It sounds like a team effort to me—and that's not a very popular idea these days.

The Leman children saw parents who were willing to share their home and family with aging parents and a great aunt who was failing both mentally and physically. We heard my dad tell of bringing home his paycheck as a teenager to help support his mother and three brothers. And we witnessed our mom agonizing over a decision that would finally place Grandma in a nursing home a few months before she died, after having shared our home for more than nine years.

In essence, we were part of a family that stuck together through good times and bad, always sharing what we had. We understood that giving was not reserved for Christmas and birthdays. It was a year-round effort on our part, often hitting where it hurt the most—in the pocketbook.

Do our children see us as adults who still listen to and consider parental advice and ideas, honoring the experience of old age? Do they see that the obedience of our childhood days is only part of honoring our parents, which carries with it the whole concept of respect for those who were originally placed in authority over us? Do they see us as independent persons whose wise decisions are enhanced by our openness to benefit from the successes and mistakes of our elders?

Our children will see a real and personal God at work in us as we honor our parents by assuming our filial responsibilities cheerfully as adults and by involving our families in the process.

"Let's help Grandma cut the lawn today."

"Wouldn't it be fun to take Grandma and Grandpa to Disneyland with us?"

"Give Grandma a call. Tell her we'll be over in a few minutes to take her to the store."

I think you get the picture.

Serving God

The Bible teaches that the Christian life is one of service and love shown to those around us. As Christian parents, we want our children to see that there is joy in serving Christ!

We need to remember that we can serve Christ wherever we are—in our homes, in the workplace, out in the community, and in the church. Serving Christ does not necessarily require becoming a member of a church committee or entering the ordained ministry.

There was a time in my life when I was overwhelmed by how much outreach and ministry were needed all around me and by how little time I had, as a young parent, to contribute. Then I realized that God could use me right where I was every day, at First Covenant Church Preschool in Jamestown, New York. When I began to pray and allow myself to be available for His use, exciting things began to happen.

I had opportunities to minister to families of young children through Bible studies in my home, an annual Vacation Bible School for preschoolers, a "Time Out" program for moms of our little ones, and get-acquainted picnics at our nearby church camp. How thrilling it was to share the love of Christ with families who became friends first and then sisters and brothers in the family of God as they gave their lives and hearts to Christ.*

Karin, Kristine, and Tom, were you watching? What did you see?

Me, Too, Mom and Dad!

Including our children when we help others creates wonderful opportunities for them to gain practical experience. Not only are we sharing special times together that will build treasured memories but we are also teaching our children what Christian living is all about.

Here are ways to do just that:

1. Bake a cake with your child and take it to the new neighbors.
2. Give a "Just Because" gift to someone other than at birthday or holiday time.
3. Baby-sit for a young couple—free of charge.
4. Prepare dinner for someone who has come home from the hospital.

---

* A note of caution is in order here. Service *to* God cannot equate or replace a relationship *with* God. For the Christian whose livelihood comes from any form of Christian ministry, this can be a dangerous trap. But all Christians—especially Christian parents—are in full-time service for God, and in our busy-ness and enthusiasm for church activities—and even parenting—we can overlook our need for the lifeline of a loving, give-and-take relationship with our Lord.

5. Include children in your visits to the nursing home. (Be sure to prepare them, gently, for what they may see.)
6. Allow your children to help fix a casserole or salad for a bereaved family. Even though they may be too young to attend calling hours or the funeral, they will have helped to offer comfort.
7. Make cards and gifts for teachers, grandparents, or shut-ins. This is a wonderful rainy-day activity.
8. Mow the lawn or rake leaves for an elderly person.
9. Pick up someone for church.

Remember, each of these service opportunities is tailor-made for casual but purposeful conversations about birth and death, loving and caring for others, and serving Jesus.

Criticism

No matter what vocational and avocational avenues we pursue in life, no matter what groups we are involved in, we are going to encounter problems. Yes, even in the church! Just when we think we've got it together and things are going great, slap! Somebody unfurls the wet blanket of controversy!

Most of us need someone with whom to relieve our frustrations and hurt by talking out whatever crisis is currently consuming us. If you're like me, you run to your mate. But be careful: When discussing such problems, it is best to stay out of earshot of the children.

Critical natures are deadly, not only for parents but also for the children who may be listening. Remember the old saying, "Little pitchers have big ears"? Children are like sponges, absorbing everything they hear. But they are not mature enough to understand that what sounds like criticism may only be intended as evaluation.

If only it were not so easy to slip into negative thinking! Remember, constructive criticism can border on just plain gossip. We need to think twice before criticizing church programming, the pastoral staff, the choir anthem, or fellow members of the Body of Christ. If we want God to be real to our children, and if we want them to believe that there is joy in serving the Lord, we need to cultivate positive thought patterns sprinkled with kind words about other people. We need to watch our attitudes; they really have a way of creeping through. Guess who catches them?

The quality of our personal relationship with Jesus Christ, our marriage relationship, and our relationships with our children—those three vital priorities for Christian parents—will crucially impact our efforts to make God real to our children. As we move through our daily lives and through the various stages of our children's lives, we will find out that if we keep priority number one in place, the others will fall into line, for the Holy Spirit will give us sensitivity to the needs of our mates and children.

He will also give us the flexibility to keep our relational priorities in proper balance. We all know that there are times in our lives—during a move to a new home or community, during the time when a child or other loved one is critically ill or dying, or during additional periods of occupational, academic, emotional, or schedule stress—when one priority (relationship) may need special emphasis, perhaps even to the temporary neglect of the others. If we are listening carefully to Him, the Holy Spirit will give us peace about the situation, guide the timing of our thoughts, actions, and words, and protect our relationships until normalcy is restored.

As we will see in the next chapter, the three relational priorities we have just discussed are inextricably intertwined with a prime parental concern: child discipline.

Questions for Thought

1. What am I doing to deepen and enhance my personal relationship with God?

2. How can I develop the childlikeness Jesus longs to see in my faith?

3. Am I applying biblical principles to everyday situations in my marriage?

4. In what ways can I reach out with God's love to children in my church and neighborhood who come from single-parent families?

5. Is my behavior giving my children a positive or negative image of God? What do I need to change?

3

Loving Discipline: The Ball Is in Your Court, Mom and Dad

Whenever a parenting program focuses on discipline, an overflow crowd is almost inevitable. In advertising terms, the market is constant—parents of all ages and stages want to know how to handle children of all ages and stages effectively!

It has been said before: First-time expectant parents are schooled in prenatal care but are virtually unprepared for parenthood. Obstetricians across the country make sure their patients understand the importance of good nutrition during pregnancy, the progressive stages of prenatal development, and the merits of sonograms and amniocentesis. Moms- and dads-to-be practice the latest techniques in getting through labor and delivery the natural way.

Once baby arrives, Mommy and Daddy enjoy a few days together in the maternity wing cuddling their new addition and deciding whom he or she looks like. They bask in the attention and admiration of visiting relatives, unwrap gifts, wonder where to put all of those lovely floral arrangements, and maybe even share a candlelight dinner for two in the quietness of a special hospital dining room.

But on homegoing day, reality hits. There will be no more nurse's aides to take the baby when he is fussy so Mom can get her sleep. Grandma and Grandpa can only stay a few days, and then. . . .

Even if first-time parents have been baby-sitters, taken child-development courses, or come from families with younger siblings or cousins, the task of caring for their own child poses plenty of uncertainties. But if those early weeks and months of physical care seem formidable, they look easy, in retrospect, once the new parent encounters the bewildering world of child discipline.

As a young parent, I often overheard members of the older generation talk about what a nice child so-and-so was and how awful someone else's youngster acted. I did so want our first child to be well behaved. To be honest, I did not want anyone to have a reason to criticize her or the way we were raising her! But like most first-time parents, we were less confident of our parenting abilities than we looked.

It did not help to realize that the pendulum of currently fashionable child-discipline theories regularly swings from one extreme to the other—from authoritarianism to permissiveness, from the perils of overprotectiveness to punishment bordering on outright child abuse. We knew there was danger at each extremity. How could we find a healthy balance? Thanks to our Christian faith, Wes and I were able to turn to God's Word, our instruction manual, for answers. As we did so, we gradually learned how to incorporate our quest for making God real to our children into the daily process of discipline.

What *Does* the Bible Say About Discipline?

The father of a five-year-old motioned me aside one morning after Sunday school class.

"Sally," he said, "when I read about disciplining children in the Old Testament, everything sounds so harsh and cruel. But the New Testament seems to promote a totally different concept of discipline—and it appears to contradict the Old Testament! How come?"

Time did not permit us to talk long that morning, but the following week we pursued the subject in detail, making lists of Old and New Testament instructions to parents. Our comparison yielded these results:

OLD TESTAMENT REFERENCES TO PARENTING	NEW TESTAMENT REFERENCES TO PARENTING
1. Actions reveal a child's character. Proverbs 21:11	1. "God's correction is always right and for our best good." Hebrews 12:10
2. Correct your children. It won't hurt them to be disciplined. Proverbs 23:13, 14	2. The results of punishment produce "a quiet growth in grace and character." Hebrews 12:11
3. Use a stick on them. They won't die. Proverbs 23:13, 14	3. Don't keep scolding and nagging your children; it will make them angry and resentful. Discipline them with love, offering suggestions and godly advice. Ephesians 6:4

4. "Punishment will keep them out of hell."
Proverbs 23:13, 14

5. Punishment will drive rebellion from a child's heart.
Proverbs 22:15

6. Scolding and spanking help a child to learn.
Proverbs 29:15

7. If you do not discipline your child in his early years, you will ruin his life.
Proverbs 19:18

8. Refusing to discipline your child "proves you don't love him."
Proverbs 13:24

9. Be prompt in your punishment.
Proverbs 13:24

10. "God is . . . pleased we are just and fair."
Proverbs 21:3

4. "It is best to listen much, speak little, and not become angry."
James 1:19, 20

5. Do not complain or argue.
Philippians 2:14

6. Your conversation should be gracious and sensible.
Colossians 4:6

7. Be careful because what you say can do enormous damage.
James 3:5

8. "Stop being mean, bad-tempered and angry. Quarreling, harsh words, and dislike of others should have no place in your lives."
Ephesians 4:31, 32

9. "Don't let the sun go down with you still angry."
Ephesians 4:26

10. "Don't be too eager to tell others their faults." We all make mistakes. Control your tongue.
James 3:1, 2

11. It is a calamity to have a rebellious child.

Proverbs 19:13

11. Be merciful, kind, gentle, and forgiving. Never hold a grudge. Let your life be guided by love. Teach Christ's words to each other. Represent the Lord Jesus in whatever you do or say.

Colossians 3:12–17

12. A man who mocked his father and despised his mother deserved a severe punishment.

Proverbs 30:17

13. During the early history of Israel the law demanded the death penalty if:
    anyone hit his father or mother.

Exodus 21:15

    anyone cursed his father or mother.

Leviticus 20:9

    a rebellious and stubborn son continued to disobey and remained a drunkard even though punished.

Deuteronomy 21:18–24

In short, the Old Testament instructions seem to major on the themes of parental authority and punishment for sin. The negative results of youthful rebellion are clearly spelled out—ruined lives, shattered relationships, and death.

The New Testament instructions also stress parental firmness but major on the importance of parents modeling the love, patience, graciousness, and forgiveness of Jesus. The positive results of loving discipline—spiritual growth, good familial relationships, self-control, and balanced perspectives on life—shine through.

Why the difference? In fact, why did a God we know to be just, yes, but loving and forgiving as well, issue the Old Testament Law in the first place, with its stringent regulations and emphasis on punishment for wrongdoing?

Because although God planned all along to send a Savior to redeem the earth from the sinful mess into which Adam and Eve's sin plunged it, He knew the time was not yet right. So He *guarded* Israel by issuing laws designed to preserve her national identity, strengthen her family units, and protect His chosen people (through whom Jesus would eventually come) from illness and the devastating consequences of disobedience. Only strong, firmly held faith in and respect for God Almighty and His laws on the part of His people could accomplish those goals in a world that wanted no part of Him. Thus, the Old Testament emphasis on the Law.

When, in God's sovereign timing, He determined that the world was ready for a Savior, He revealed the fullness and completeness of His love for us in Jesus. Jesus delivered us from the need for the Law and took all the punishment we deserved for our rebellion against God, dying on Calvary so we could be forgiven and live our lives in fellowship with Him.

But, as missionary/writer Oswald Chambers comments, Jesus did not die on the cross for us out of sympathy. He was actually "made . . . to be sin for us" (2 Corinthians 5:21 NIV). In His death our sin is exchanged for His righteousness.

"That Christ died for me, therefore, I go scot free, is never taught in the New Testament," says Chambers in his classic devotional *My Utmost for His Highest* (Dodd, Mead, and Company, 1935). "It is not Christ *for* me unless I am determined to have Christ *formed* in me."

What does all this have to do with child discipline? Just as the Mosaic Law *safeguarded*, *guided*, and *corrected* the Israelites through the perils of history until the time was right for Jesus to come, so loving discipline from Christ-transformed parents can *safeguard*, *guide*, and *correct* a child until he or she comes to see the need for Christ's righteousness to be formed within, through personal acceptance of His sacrifice and through the indwelling of the Holy Spirit.

New Testament parents are free to discipline their children—*in love*. Removing love from discipline equals punishment—something you do *to* the child, not *for* the child.

Sounds Like a Tall Order!

Remember, perfect Christian parents do not exist, because we are imperfect human beings to begin with. But as each of us cultivates that top-priority relationship with Christ and allows His Holy Spirit to conform us to His image, we will begin to take on His attributes. Study the following list, picturing how His attributes, lived out in each of us, can help us to discipline our children in love.

Jesus Christ:

- has authority over us
- gives us freedom of choice

- holds us accountable for our actions/choices
- is firm and honest
- confronts issues as needed
- is a wonderful teacher
- loved us first and loves us unconditionally, just as we are
- is compassionate
- is just and fair
- is our comforter
- prays for us
- honored His mother and provided for her care
- forgives and forgets
- is concerned for the inner person
- is concerned about the spirit, not the letter, of the law
- is consistent, unchanging
- gave His all for us
- listens to us

Wanted: Disciplined Parents

Some of you may remember trying to potty train your first child. You put little Susie on the potty at regular intervals throughout the day and hoped she would experience the thrill of success before long. Remember watching intently for distress signals like squirming or jumping up and down? Perhaps you suddenly realized, one day, that the house was just too quiet. You looked around and there was Susie, standing in the corner concentrating on a potty break. You whisked her upstairs to the bathroom—hoping to make it in time.

Who was potty trained? Certainly not Susie! But because *you* were disciplined and consistent in your efforts, they eventually paid off.

The same principle applies to loving child discipline. When parents, empowered by the Holy Spirit, put their lives in order spiritually, curb their own bad habits, and model behavior that is both biblically and socially acceptable—in short, when parents discipline *themselves*—many child behavior problems evaporate, and others shrink to manageable size. Those that remain are less stressful to deal with because God's wisdom and creativity are there for the asking.

A Word About Spanking

Spanking has long been a point of controversy among parents, grandparents, psychologists, teachers, and others concerned with children's issues. Each of us has our own ideas as to how often, if at all, how hard, with what, and for what reasons a spanking should be administered. I will forego any lengthy discussion on these points. The experts have said it all, in numerous secular and Christian books and articles, which are widely available.

I must simply reiterate that the primary focus of New Testament teaching on parenting seems to be the application of loving discipline by parents who are controlled by the Holy Spirit. I am concerned that some Bible-believing Christians fail to see discipline in its proper scriptural context and hold to some Old Testament passages as license to abuse their children physically and/or verbally. Such behavior is entirely unbiblical.

What if I Lose Control?

If dealing with a particular behavioral problem tries your patience to the point where you feel you are losing control, leave the scene as quickly as possible. Walk into another room, place the child in his or her room—just get away and calm down. Never place your child in jeopardy.

Remember: Parents—Christian and non-Christian—are human. We all lose it from time to time.

In his excellent book *Becoming a Whole Family* (Word Books, 1975), Presbyterian pastor John Huffman describes an incident in which he and his wife, Anne, had an abnormally harsh argument. Following a verbal battle, he and Anne usually went to their room to pray together and apologize, but on this occasion Huffman realized their three-year-old daughter, Suzanne, had observed the hostile exchange.

"Instead of going to our bedroom with Anne," says Huffman, "I turned and said, 'Suzanne, Daddy's been a bad boy. Daddy needs a spanking, doesn't he?' Her eyes became big as saucers, but the shocked expression quickly changed to an ear-to-ear smile. Her response was, 'Daddy naughty, too?' "

When we have lost control and treated our spouses or children unfairly, we are the ones who need the spanking to make us straighten up. We are the ones who need to ask for God's forgiveness, as well as our children's. Seeing our willingness to admit our imperfections and ask for God's help in changing our behavior gives them yet another glimpse of how to relate honestly to the real, down-to-earth God we love and worship.

This isn't fair, you're saying. You thought this chapter was about *child* discipline.

Hang on—we are getting to that. But first let's observe how one mother applied some God-empowered self-discipline and improved her children's lives and characters, too.

Poor Emily

Emily's world seemed to be disintegrating around her. For over a year her husband's work schedule had taken him out of town during the week, so Saturdays and Sundays—crammed with errands, church, and community functions—were their only time together. The children were two years apart and seemed to demand every ounce of her energy. Try as she would, she could not get both children to nap at the same time, so a break for some personal space was nearly impossible. Screaming at the kids had become a regular part of her day.

On top of everything else, the kitchen floor was always sticky, the ironing was piled as high as Mt. Everest, dishes were stacked in piles beside the sink, and toys were strewn from one end of the house to the other. Emily had worn maternity clothes for so long she felt just plain dowdy, and her old jeans and tops from prebaby days did not fit. In spite of her longing to be a loving Christian wife and mother and to make God real to her children, nostalgia for her free-to-be-me fashion-plate era as a corporate executive secretary overwhelmed her.

Fortunately Emily recognized that she needed God's help to discipline herself to succeed in her roles. Guided by her strong (if temporarily neglected) Christian faith, she began to make some changes.

First Steps.

Setting the alarm clock for forty-five minutes earlier was one of Emily's first steps in rearranging her life. Using that time for Bible reading, prayer, personal hygiene, and an uninterrupted bowl of Cheerios and cup of coffee enabled her to greet the children calmly when they did tumble out of bed.

The newly awakened perceptions gained from quiet time with the Lord helped Emily to recognize some of the dynamics that had turned her life into a pressure cooker. Weather conditions, financial strains, undone housework, shaky relationships in her extended family, a poor self-concept, fatigue, excessive church and community responsibilities, and the fact that she was, for all practical purposes, a single parent five days a week had all combined to cloud her physical, emotional, mental, and spiritual responses. She could see that the same pressures were having a trickle-down effect on her children's reactions, as well.

Time Out.

Emily could not reverse weather patterns or adjust her husband's work schedule, but she decided to make changes where she could bring more harmony into her family's life.

One such area was her poor self-concept, compounded by fatigue. Far from being a selfish person, Emily realized that a small investment of time in herself would also yield dividends for her children.

After talking things over with her husband, Emily decided to stretch the budget to include a few inexpensive at-home outfits and a couple of new dresses for church. A shopping trip followed by a quiet dinner for two at a local restaurant the next weekend gave her a fresh outlook. An unexpected benefit was the fun the children had relating to a new babysitter.

Another time-out strategy Emily discovered was to trade child-care favors with another mother, thus enabling herself to get out for an occasional lunch date with a friend. She also discovered the existence of a play group in the neighborhood, where mothers and children spent a morning together with different toys and the stimulation of peers.

The House Looks Like Something Hit It!

Another changeable area in Emily's life was the housework situation. A trip to the local discount department store paid off big. Plastic crates and covered boxes were just what she needed to separate, organize, and store the children's toys. Emily discovered that the newly ordered toy area actually invited her children to entertain themselves as they discovered long-forgotten favorites. Rotating playthings (by storing some and periodically producing a "new" box of toys) did wonders to relieve the perennial problem of boredom.

Emily saw, however, that she could not expect her very young children to keep the play area neat. So, taking advantage of what they had heard about cooperation on "Sesame Street" and other educational children's programming, she made up a silly "helping" song and turned picking-up time into a family affair. She knew that as the children matured and habits became ingrained, she would be able to gradually back out of the picture.

The same method worked with other household tasks as well. Folding washcloths and towels was good practice for little fingers, and delivering clean, freshly folded clothes to various rooms was not beyond the little ones' capabilities. Drying dishes, stuffing dirty laundry in the hamper, and straightening dining room chairs were also child-sized tasks. And one of Emily's small assistants was a whiz with a vacuum cleaner!

Yes, allowing the children to help required more of Emily's patience, but the togetherness and newly instilled attitudes of helpfulness and pride in accomplishment were worth it. And it did not hurt that the children began to value their playtimes more highly!

We could go on, but I think we can see that Emily's attempts to get her own life in order were yielding big dividends in organization, peace of mind, and a happier day-to-day existence. Loving child discipline was becoming a natural function of Emily's daily routine, because she herself was more disciplined—and her husband and other family members noticed the changes in both mother and children. Most important, Emily's little ones were watching as their mother allowed her faith in God to make practical changes in her life.

Solving Some Specific Discipline Problems: Be Prepared!

We are almost ready to discuss some specific discipline problems that occur in nearly every normal family setting. But before we do, let me share a couple of guidelines.

First, it is usually best to deal with behavioral situations as they occur throughout the day. Forget the idea of waiting until Daddy (or Mommy) gets home from work. No child needs that threat hanging over his or her head.

Of course, sharing decisions on family policies with your mate is important. But if he or she, on arriving home, disagrees with a disciplinary action or decision you have made during the day, discuss it when the children are in bed or otherwise out of earshot. Parents need to present a united front, and sometimes it takes time and privacy to hammer one out!

Second, prepare to apply loving child discipline by having some idea of what to expect from your children at particular ages. Several good books on age-appropriate responses are listed on page 27. Talking to other parents will help, too.

It is easy to expect more of the oldest child or of a child who is big for his or her age. At the other end of the spectrum, it is easy to let things slide with the youngest. (Do we parents tire out, or do we just become more relaxed as time goes by?) It is easy to baby those little ones, so be careful. Never do for a child what he can do for himself.

Just remember that children are individually fashioned by God. No two are exactly alike.

Now, on to those hard-to-call plays.

But They're Into Everything!

Sure little kids get into things! They are naturally curious. They learn by exploring.

It is hard to keep small fingers from touching all those lovely knickknacks around our homes. Should we childproof a house completely by clearing every table? Or should we leave everything as it was before Junior came on the scene?

I took the middle ground and left some items out because I wanted my children to learn that there were some things we do *not* play with. It turned out to be good training for those times when I took them to visit in other homes.

There are some children with whom this approach will not work: They are just dying to get their hands on what they are forbidden to touch. Play it by ear. If one method does not work, be disciplined and flexible enough to try another.

It might help to allow your child to sit on the sofa and carefully hold the pink glass heirloom dish Aunt Mary left you. After all, it *is* fun to peek through—see how pink everything looks? Let this be a special treat; it may end the temptation to touch. Then again, it may not. Be patient: Your little one is learning to respect his or her home and other people's belongings.

It is important to take a good long look around the house to ensure that everything hazardous to young children is out of reach. Install safety devices such as drawer and cupboard door latches and electrical outlet covers. They not only protect kids—they also prevent some battles by removing temptation! Remember to check out the houseplants, too; some are poisonous and may need to be sent to Grandma's until the children are older.

Some parents spend hundreds of dollars on toys for their children, only to find they prefer to play with pots, pans, and plastic kitchenware. If possible, place such unbreakables in a drawer or cupboard and let little ones get into it! They would far rather play on the floor, right beside Mommy, than be exiled to a second-floor playroom. Just think of all the fun possibilities for sharing ideas about God, daily life, and relationships as you work side by side!

He Runs From Morning 'Til Night

Sound familiar? Provide a balance in his daily routine. Be sure quiet activities are included at various times through the day, especially before naptime and bedtime.

Regular outings, offering fresh air and exercise, are musts for little ones, too. Let them run off all that extra energy outdoors. One mother designated certain activities (bouncing balls, running, wrestling matches, and general roughhousing) as outside play; if her children began any of those activities indoors, her quiet reminder helped them to choose whether they wanted to continue outside or pick another pastime.

If a child simply cannot seem to settle down, holding him firmly but gently may help. Tell him why you are holding him. This is also a good time to express loving reassurances. A "time out" chair may be effective if it is not overused.

Will She Ever Learn to Share?

Sharing is an age-related developmental skill. All too often I have seen young parents berate a one- or two-year-old harshly for failing to share—when the child has no understanding whatsoever about the concept of sharing. His or her little world revolves around self, and while that needs to change, the change must come gradually and in accordance with his or her mental, emotional, and physical readiness.

Here are two specific strategies that will work miracles in helping children mature in their sharing skills:

1. Keep a portable timer handy, or use the one on the kitchen stove. If problems develop over a particular toy, tell the children that you are going to set the timer for so many minutes. Explain that one child may play with the toy until the timer rings, and then he or she must pass it on to the next person. Then set the timer.

When it goes off, simply say, "The bell says it's Jimmy's turn now." If they whine or fuss, pleasantly but firmly suggest that you may have to "retire" the toy for an hour if they can't cooperate.

Be firm, and the children will soon realize that the bell has the final word. What a wonderful way to get the parent off the hook! Better yet, children are learning to make decisions and choosing their own consequences.

2. If guests are coming, plan ahead with your child and discuss which toys he and his friend would like to play with. Also discuss which toys might be too fragile to be shared and put them out of sight.

Sometimes we need duplicate toys like bubble sets or Barbie dolls, but let's face it, we cannot buy two of everything, and it would not be good training for our children if we did!

If sharing is a problem for your child, acknowledge the frustration he or she is feeling:

"I know how much you want to play with the car, Billy, but let's let Michael finish using it. Then it will be your turn." With practice, a timer, and firmness on your part, you may be able, a few minutes later, to say, "Thank you for sharing the car with Michael, Billy. You are a kind friend."

Remember, sharing is difficult for younger children. Getting together with playmates is a real learning experience—part of their "work" as little ones. Not everything will run smoothly, and they are going to need lots of practice. But if we as parents and grandparents have a plan and stick to it (self-discipline, remember?), sharing *will* begin to happen.

Say What You Mean and Follow Through

It was church softball league night. Mom took the twins to the park to watch Daddy play. She asked the twins to stay in the safe area behind the backstop. But they ignored her directions and the warning that if she had to speak to them once more, they would all go home.*

As soon as she saw them out of bounds again, Mom calmly took one twin by one hand and the other twin by the other

---

* Note: Most experts in the field of child discipline suggest that parents train their youngsters to respond after the *first* verbal instruction, using firm discipline if they do not. Children quickly learn the limits of a parent's patience and routinely stretch it to the limit: "She always calls at least three times before she means it!"

and started for the car. En route to the parking area they spotted the playground.

"Please, Mommy?" they wheedled.

"I'm sorry, but you didn't listen to Mommy. Now we have to go home. Next time we come I think you'll remember to play where you're supposed to play," she replied.

Mom wasn't any more anxious to go home than the twins were. It was a beautiful summer evening, and she had been looking forward to watching the game and visiting with her friends. But her self-discipline and loving child discipline paid off—the next game they lasted for all seven innings!

Say what you mean and follow through. God does!

How You Say It *Does* Make a Difference

It helps to speak positively to young children. "Remember that we walk in the house, Jenny. We can run when we're outside."

Save *no* for really important issues and it will mean more to a child. I used to wonder why *no* was one of the first words in any child's vocabulary. Then I stopped to count how many times we parents use the word during the day! Remember, we are being watched—and imitated.

Did you notice how the mother in the previous illustration employed her voice as a helpful disciplinary tool? She kept it calm and matter-of-fact, even in the midst of a trying disciplinary situation. (No, this is not easy, but self-discipline makes perfect—almost!) Strengthened by a firm resolve that her children's training and welfare came before her own pleasure, her refusal to lose control went a long way toward convincing two little people that she meant business and could not be manipulated.

If you really want your child to listen, or if his or her tone of voice is consistently loud and strident, try whispering.

Defusing Potential Areas of Conflict

Laughing *with* our children (never *at* them) goes a long way toward defusing potential parent-child conflict. And laughing at ourselves helps, too.

Three-year-old Jimmy's table manners needed improvement. Rather than lecture him on the proper use of a napkin, his mom questioned him in a fun-loving way:

"Jimmy, do we wipe our mouths with our sleeves?"

"No," Jimmy replied with a giggle.

"Do we wipe our mouths with the backs of our hands?"

"No," Jimmy replied more loudly, laughing out loud. "You're silly, Mom."

"Well, how *do* we wipe our mouths?" asked Mom.

"With our napkins!" Jimmy shouted.

"Right!" said Mom.

Beware: Such tomfoolery can backfire—but when it does it usually adds much-needed humor to our all-too-serious lives.

One day at the preschool where I work there was a lot of commotion in the playhouse corner. Annie was thoroughly enjoying throwing things around the kitchen.

"Annie, let's pick up the toys under the table. I bet your mommy doesn't throw things on the floor at home," I said with a smile.

"Uh-huh!" Annie nodded knowingly. "She throws the broccoli!"

Another method for defusing potential conflict comes from learning to look ahead, to anticipate children's probable next moves.

Mom, Katie, and Ben had just been to visit Grandma at the hospital. Now the children were racing toward the elevator, and Mom, knowing from experience what was about to happen, decided to intervene.

"Katie! Ben!" she called. "I hear the elevator coming. Which door do you think will open first?" Making a game out of waiting for the elevator distracted the children from a potential hassle over who got to push the button and kept them quiet, too.

Loving child discipline—New Testament style—involves the prevention of problems, not just their resolution. Parental self-discipline and even an elemental understanding of what happens when in the development of a child's personality can stop much behavioral acting out before it starts. In the following chapters we will discuss other creative ways to make God real to our children that also help to prevent and resolve difficult behavioral situations.

Questions for Thought

1. Does the way I discipline my children resemble Old Testament or New Testament examples (*see* chart on pages 60–62)? Is it a balance of both? How can I be more like Jesus in relating to my children?

2. Are there specific areas in which self-discipline on my part could improve our family life?

3. How can I use my voice, choose my words, and follow through in actions to create an atmosphere of effective, loving discipline that both prevents and resolves problems?

4

Making God Real Through
Improved Communication Skills

Miss Lynn and her class of four-year-olds had worked long and hard getting ready for their Christmas program. They had made gifts for their parents and planned a party with sherbet punch, frosted cut-out cookies, and pretty, child-decorated napkins. Today was the day, and the children fairly danced about the classroom in excitement.

When it was time for the program to begin, the children took their places on the rug at Miss Lynn's feet. A helper opened the door, and in came the moms and dads, who managed to sit quite comfortably in child-sized chairs scattered around the cheerful classroom.

After a minute or two of smiling, waving, and reassuring themselves of their parents' seating arrangements, the children were ready to sing. And sing they did, right from the tips of their toes.

But over half of the parents were not listening. They were chatting with one another, completely oblivious to the program. What did their inattention communicate to their children? That they did not appreciate their children's efforts? Or care about their feelings? That all of Miss Lynn's planning and preparation were inconsequential? Whatever happened to plain, old-fashioned good manners and respect?

"We Don't Get No Respect!"

Rodney Dangerfield may be right: Respect for human beings—not to mention God!—does seem to be in short supply in modern America. Many adults are very willing to blame it on a younger generation that often is, admittedly, disrespectful. But such adults fail to understand that the younger generation simply imitates what it sees. Parents and grandparents who routinely talk and whisper during a children's program or who march out of a school concert immediately after *their* child performs should not be surprised when children wander randomly in and out of auditoriums. Adults who offer loud and scornful criticism of their own superiors have little right to scold when they hear students deriding teachers. And parents and grandparents who deny their family members a listening ear should not be shocked and angry at a child who walks out of the room before Dad has finished lecturing.

How carefully we parents need to think through and monitor our everyday verbal and nonverbal responses to each other and to our children! In this chapter we will examine several biblical, elementary principles of communication that, built into family life, almost automatically teach mutual respect by example. Ignoring them can erode our children's respect for us, for others, and for property.

After all, how can our children learn to respect, love, and communicate with an unseen God if they do not first learn respect, love, and good communication skills in the home?

Principle Number One: Practice Intentional Listening.

According to the *American Heritage Dictionary*, the word *listen* implies "making an effort" to hear something, "paying attention." Unfortunately both word and practice have fallen into disuse in all too many present-day homes, drowned out by the worries of daily life and a deluge of electronic devices and frantic activities. Consequently, while it is technically repetitious, I have added the adjective *intentional* to help us grasp anew this first, vitally important principle in establishing effective family communication lines.

What, then, is intentional listening? My dictionary suggests that an intention is "a plan of action." And that is just what intentional listening is—a *plan of action* to help us communicate better with God, our mates, and our children. It is listening with a clear-cut purpose in mind.

Conversely, intentional listening is *not* the haphazard, absentminded, halfhearted pretense that so often passes for listening in our homes. We will talk more about that later, but let's look at what our instructional manual, the Bible, has to say about intentional listening. As usual, its advice is logical and on target, with practical tips for the concerned parent.

Intentional listening—to God. In chapter two we cited the Christian parent's number one priority as being his or her relationship to God through Jesus Christ. We need, then, to apply the principle of intentional listening in *this* relationship before it can operate effectively in relationships with our children.

Christian growth in communication or any other area does not take place as we resolve, over and over, to do better. It only happens as we allow God's Holy Spirit to speak to us through His Word—and that involves intentional listening.

Then the Holy Spirit can remind us of His Word when we need it most, even in the midst of major and minor family crises.

The fifth chapter of the Book of Ecclesiastes says:

> Guard your steps when you go to the house of God. Go near to listen rather than to offer the sacrifice of fools, who do not know that they do wrong. Do not be quick with your mouth, do not be hasty in your heart to utter anything before God. God is in heaven and you are on earth, so let your words be few.
>
> Ecclesiastes 5:1, 2 NIV

In the Gospel of John, chapter 10, verse 27, Jesus says, "My sheep listen to my voice" (NIV). And James, writing to Hebrew believers, cautioned, "Do not merely listen to the word, and so deceive yourselves. Do what it says" (1:22 NIV). Intentional listening to God is important! But notice two qualities that seem to accompany intentional listening: restraint of our speech and obedience to God's direction.

"Do not be quick . . . hasty . . . to utter anything before God. . . . Let your words be few," says the writer of Ecclesiastes. And from the Book of Proverbs come these additional comments along the same line: "Let the wise listen and add to their learning," (1:5 NIV), and "He who answers before listening—that is his folly and his shame" (18:13 NIV). How often I foolishly spend my prayer time doing all the talking— and none of the listening! Quietness before Him, spent in meditation on His Word or just in waiting, can yield ideas, inspiration, and creativity beyond our imaginations and our own earthly wisdom.

But once we have listened, we need to obey. Has God

given me an insight regarding how I react (or overreact) to a child or mate? I need the Holy Spirit to help me ask that person's forgiveness and to remind me to respond differently next time. Has He suggested some loving gesture I can make to ease a youngster's hurt? I need to act on it.

Here it is again—the power of example. As we parents intentionally listen to God and act on what we hear, our children will begin to see the results in our lives—and in their own! As a result, they may be more receptive to what we say about God.

Intentional listening—to our mates. It would be a real temptation to skip right into discussing intentional listening to our children. But we need to pause for a brief reminder that this same principle applies to that number-two priority for the Christian parent—the relationship with his or her mate. The biblical passages relating to marriage are strong in their support for an institution God *created for our benefit.* Why, then, are we so prone to disparage or dismiss our mate's comments, feelings, thoughts, and advice? To ignore the counsel and friendship God wanted us to enjoy as a result of marriage?

"She's always nagging me," a husband claims. "He puts me down," sobs a wife. Intentional listening is one of the best ways to love a mate because it validates his or her importance in our eyes and offers respect. (It also validates my own good judgment in choosing such a superior person with whom to spend my life!) When my eyes and my body language reassure my mate that I care enough to listen to his inmost concerns, real communication begins to happen on other levels, as well. But when I jump in with unthinking advice before I have really heard what my mate has to say, the verse from Proverbs 18 suggests I am apt to get embarrassed!

Remember: The children are watching. Intentional listening to them will not ring true if they see Mommy and Daddy failing to show the same courteous treatment to each other.

Intentional listening—to our children. Are we listening, you ask? How can we help it? All our young children do is shout questions, day in and day out. Our ears are worn-out from listening!

But are we listening *intentionally*? All of those "whys" flow from bright, curious, eager-to-learn minds. A child's endless questions can be amusing and challenging. I agree that they can also be a source of aggravation, especially when we are tired, busy, or anxious. But if we show our annoyance too frequently, the doors of communication may begin to close.

Four-year-old Jimmy and his dad were watching a baseball game on television, something they usually enjoyed doing together. But tonight was different; Jimmy's questions seemed to shoot like bullets out of a machine gun.

"Dad, how old is Nolan Ryan?"

"Dad, is he married?

"Dad, what's his batting average?

"Dad, do you think the Rangers will win?

"Dad . . . ?"

Finally Jimmy's long-suffering father uttered the time-honored parental reply—which unfortunately has shut down all too many potentially meaningful discussions.

"Jimmy, you ask too many questions!"

Kids really do deserve answers, even if we have to say, "I don't know, but I'll try to find out." It's one important way they learn. Their queries may stop if we choose not to answer. And someone else may step in—with the wrong information.

Yes, sometimes it is tough being a parent, and we feel like stamping our feet and shouting, "Will you *please* be quiet?" If, like me, you have ever said exactly that, a big hug and, "I'm sorry, Mommy's really tired tonight," go a long way toward smoothing ruffled feelings.

And, yes, sometimes our desire for peace and quiet is justified. At such times try a simple, "Honey, Mommy's ears are tired tonight. I want to answer your questions, but I need to rest awhile first, maybe until the news is over. Then we'll have a good talk!" Just remember—it's your job to follow through. They'll be waiting!

Kids get frustrated, too! Our failure to listen cuts deeper than depriving our children of interesting information. It can frustrate and discourage them, also, damaging their fragile self-esteem. Acknowledging the importance of their curiosity shows our respect for them as persons.

It was summertime. All the relatives were together for a picnic supper, and four-year-old Paul was sitting beside his mother, listening as she talked with Uncle Joe.

"Mom!" Paul interrupted.

Mom kept on talking and didn't even look his way.

"Mom!" Paul persisted.

Mom kept on eating, now giving her attention to Uncle Joe's wife, Aunt Sara.

"Mom!" Paul gently tapped her arm.

"Mom!" Now he was tugging at her sleeve.

"Yes, dear?" Mom finally answered.

By the time dinner was over, a relative observed that little Paul had called his mother's name twenty-seven times throughout the meal.

Yes, Paul wanted some attention.

Yes, he probably had something special he wanted to say.

Yes, Mom was tuning him out.

Yes, that is a good way to strangle a relationship with a child, if the pattern continues.

One of my graduate school professors told our class about a little girl whose mother consistently offered token answers and absentminded "uh-huhs" to her attempts to ask questions and converse. Finally the child exclaimed in disgust, "Mommy, you're not listening with your face!"

I'm glad God listens with His face! He focuses directly on our specific needs; He's never in a hurry; He is always there for us, waiting patiently. The Bible says that the God who watches over us neither slumbers nor sleeps. We can't imagine *Him* tuning us out while He reads the newspaper! And even though we often ignore His loving advice, He continues to respect our free will and to love us enough to accept our apologies and reinstate us to fellowship with Him after we have blown it.

Children can understand the reality of a loving, listening, heavenly Father if they have parents who show respect for their children by listening with their faces!

Principle Number Two: Begin Early to Talk With Your Children.

Almost all parents talk *to* their children, but Christian parents need to make a concerted effort to talk *with* their children.

The biblical precedent and principle are clear. From the earliest days of the world, God has longed for communication with human beings. He was apparently accustomed to walks in the Garden with Adam and Eve, and their recorded dialogue implies a meaningful give-and-take between the Creator and His creatures. (*See* Genesis 1–4.)

The pattern continued throughout the Old Testament, as God repeatedly initiated conversations with those who loved Him—and even with those who did not. He never forced Himself on anyone; He sometimes withdrew temporarily if their response was unwelcoming. But He persisted in reaching out.

We need to reach out, also, to include children in our everyday conversations. They can contribute so much to family fun and to the family store of knowledge! Our receptivity to and desire for their input will reinforce their feelings of significance in our families and will boost their self-esteem as they sense that their comments are of value to us, their parents and grandparents. An additional by-product may be the growth of their verbal skills, so highly valued in today's academic world.

I do not mean to imply that children should be the center of attention at all times and completely dominate every conversation. We need balance in this area: Some subject matter, time, and context can be legitimately set aside for adults only.

But current statistics tell us that meaningful daily conversation between parents and children can be measured, on the average, in *minutes*. As youngsters become independent and spend more time in structured activities outside the home, time for conversation can and often does cease to exist, especially if comfortable relationships have not been previously established. Loving, matter-of-fact, intelligent conversation (not baby talk) with small infants and toddlers as we work around the house or do errands around town lays the groundwork for the solid avenues of give-and-take communication so necessary to healthy parent-child relationships and respect. We can't begin too early!

*Principle Number Three: Whenever Possible, Communicate
Positively, Not Negatively.*

The Bible warns us in James 3:5 of the enormous damage
the tongue can do. The fourth chapter of the Book of Colossians, verse 6, suggests that our conversation should be gracious as well as sensible. And in his letter to the Ephesians the
apostle Paul tells parents, "Don't keep on scolding and nagging your children, making them angry and resentful. Rather,
bring them up with the loving discipline the Lord himself
approves, with suggestions and godly advice" (6:4).

All of us who work with children need to monitor what
comes out of our mouths. Teachers and parents who try the
negative approach are dismayed when their charges continue
to wiggle and wrestle. Notice the difference:

"Now children, stop slouching. Sit up straight and tall. And
stop that talking—it's story time!"

Or: "Jenny is ready for our story. Her hands are so nice and
quiet in her lap. And I like the way Spencer is sitting. I can
tell he's ready to listen."

One by one the children begin to settle down. Hearing a
teacher or parent compliment their peers, they want to be
noticed, too.

Positive suggestions directed to young children bring results. That is why the following statements, spoken naturally
and at appropriate times, trigger positive responses within the
hearts of young children:

"God made all the trees and flowers. He made so many
beautiful things for us to enjoy. Isn't that wonderful?"

"God made you special. He loves you. He loves everybody.
He wants to be our friend."

Who wouldn't respond to a God like that?

It is so easy to fall into the negatives trap. Once in it is possible, but very difficult, to get out. With Holy Spirit-inspired common sense (a result of some intentional listening to God), we can learn to avoid making our children angry and resentful.

One sure way to discourage and embarrass a child of any age, for example, is to talk publicly, in his presence, about his problems. Have you ever felt that people were acting as if you weren't even there? Kids have feelings, too. If you need advice on handling a child's problem, seek it from books, close friends with parenting expertise, or a pastor or other counselor. But show family solidarity by keeping such discussions private. Broadcasting a child's difficulties to one and all violates his or her trust in you as a confidante. Our children deserve our respect and loyalty, and if we show it toward them, they will be more likely to return the compliment as a matter of course.

Saving *no* for really important issues is another way to avoid arousing unnecessary childish or teen anger and to keep conversations about everyday decisions from turning into the bitter arguments that are so discouraging to children. Many children and young people hear *no* so often it becomes meaningless. Even worse, their homes routinely feel like major battlegrounds instead of nurturing, loving environments.

If parents know their own limits, respect their own needs, and accord the same respect to other family members, children will usually be less demanding. They already know what family policy is. And children who have learned from early experience that their parents are willing to discuss schedules and activities reasonably are often more willing to negotiate themselves.

One more thought about monitoring our mouths: How careful are we to lubricate the gears of our everyday lives with generous doses of genuine verbal and facial gratitude? Everyone needs to feel appreciated, and children are no exception. We need to say thank you when family members perform even small household tasks. We need to show that we are grateful for steps saved or shared thoughts and love. We need to tell our mates and children we love them—and tell them often. And we need to turn the corners of our mouths *up*—frequently.

The Bible indicates that a grateful spirit, or a spirit of thanksgiving, is precious to God and actually helps us to assume a frame of mind for communicating with Him. (*See* Psalms 95:2, 100:4, 116:17; Jonah 2:9; Philippians 4:6; Colossians 2:6, 7.) Teaching our children, by example, to incorporate a grateful spirit into their relationships with others will eventually help them to appreciate and relate more intimately to the God "who richly provides us with everything for our enjoyment" (1 Timothy 6:17 NIV).

Principle Number Four: Avoid Missed Signals and Misunderstandings.

When children are preschoolers, they take things very literally. Two simple strategies can help us to avoid misunderstandings with our little ones and/or missing their signals.

1. We must say what we mean.   Adults gain a vast repertoire of cliches and phrases over the years that helps them to communicate meaning without long explanations. But children must encounter such coded language, at some point, for the first time. Caring parents and grandparents will take time to explain what such colloquialisms mean, thus avoiding misunderstandings and enriching the child's vocabulary and cultural knowledge.

I remember apologizing to my class of three-year-olds one day when I knew I was coming down with laryngitis: "I'm sorry, boys and girls, but I can't sing very well today. I have a little frog in my throat."

The children made no comments at the time, but the next day young Amanda's mother told me how worried Amanda had been. Yes, she had thought I had a *real* frog in my throat. No matter how the mother tried, she could not convince Amanda otherwise. I wish that mother had called me at home; I would have made a house call to alleviate Amanda's worries! And I wish I had used the opportunity to explain and laugh with the children about such a funny expression!

Teachers', parents', and grandparents' words influence children profoundly, and we need to watch what we say. Adults frequently tease little children inappropriately, sometimes causing them great distress. How often have you heard a parent threaten, jokingly or angrily, "I'm going to lock you in the closet if you don't stop doing that"? Or, "Hurry up or we'll leave without you."

"Lock me in the closet?" "Leave without me?" How frightening!

And what about the times when we do not realize our children are listening? One little boy's teacher asked him if he knew where God lived.

"In the bathroom," came the confident reply.

"Why do you think God lives in the bathroom?" asked the puzzled teacher.

"Because I heard my daddy pounding on the bathroom door and calling, 'My Lord, are you still in there?' "

Funny? Yes, it is—but revealing, too. Misunderstandings and missed signals can have unfortunate repercussions in the lives of small children and lay a shaky foundation for the exchange of trusting confidences later on.

2. Offer simple, appropriate explanations when necessary, and ask questions to be sure children understand what you have said.

We can often avoid misunderstandings with our children by confronting confusing or frightening situations with honest explanations tailored to their ages and maturity levels.

When four-year-old Ryanne's ninety-five-year-old great-grandfather died, her parents gently told their children the truth, including what they thought the children could understand about death and eternal life. But they did not know that Ryanne mistook the title "Grandpa" to mean *her* grandpa, not her *father's* grandpa. Ryanne's mother did think it was a bit odd that Ryanne expressed so much grief in the succeeding days over the loss of someone she hardly knew. In all the busy-ness of getting ready for the family gathering, however, she brushed such thoughts aside.

On the day of the funeral, though, Ryanne's confusion became clear when she walked into a room after the service and there sat her grandpa! When he invited her to sit on his lap, usually a favorite spot, Ryanne refused. Turning to her parents, she said, "I thought you told me Grandpa died."

The lesson for parents? We need to be sure to ask loving, gentle questions that will help us to understand our children's perceptions of our feelings, explanations, and ideas. How many unhappy scenes this simple precaution could avoid both with little ones and teenagers! How many nightmares and hurts we could prevent!

The burden falls on us as parents to take the time to communicate *accurately* with our children. Doing so in the early years will ease the generation gap immensely as our children approach adolescence.

Principle Number Five: Actions Speak Louder Than Words.

It was a lazy Saturday afternoon, and Matt and Chuck had just returned from the movies. Entering Matt's room, they were stunned to see that pictures of his favorite rock stars had been replaced with two posters, one proclaiming "Reaching Your Potential" and the other stating "Readers Are Winners." In addition, photos of Matt's parents, baby brother, and grandparents had been substituted for the snapshots of friends that had been tucked into the frame of his mirror.

"Boy, was Matt mad," Chuck told his mom later. "He was ready to leave home!"

Can we blame him? Matt's parents' behavior conveyed a total lack of respect for their son's privacy, not to mention his feelings. We cannot know what efforts Matt's folks had made to communicate their concerns about his taste in music, his grades, or his friends prior to the redecorating job, but obviously there were some short circuits in the parent-child relationship. And in acting so drastically, and apparently without warning, this well-intentioned mom and dad had only confirmed their son's feelings that they could not or did not want to understand him.

Our actions do speak louder than our words. When we ask a child to help with a household task and then do it for him, or redo it after he leaves the room, we are conveying the message that his best efforts are not good enough. Discouragement sets in, and pretty soon the shrug of a child's shoulder or a sulky look will greet our requests for assistance.

When we insist that our children treat the church as God's house but grumble and complain in their hearing about having to raise money for a new roof for the sanctuary or better-quality linoleum for the rest rooms, we shouldn't be surprised when they show a low level of respect by climbing on the altar rails or leaving trails of soda and potato chips after youth group meetings.

Children and young people imitate what they see. If they are taught early in life that Mom respects Dad and Dad respects Mom, their respect for Mom and Dad will develop naturally. If Mom and Dad treat other family members with courtesy, so will their children. If Mom and Dad take as good care of God's house as they do their own, by picking up after activities, pitching in on church cleanup day, and giving generously to special projects, young people will, too.

Kids will be kids—they will have their share of outbursts (don't we, as adults?), run in the church aisles, and speak unkindly to little friends and big ones alike. But as a wise father once said, "If a child tries something once, he is normal. If he tries it a second time, it's the parent's fault." Our actions—in modeling respect for God, others, and property and in dealing swiftly, kindly, but firmly with misbehavior—will let our children know that we act on what we say.

Principle Number Six: Have Patience.

Some adults throw the word *immature* at the younger set like an accusation. What they mean is that kids are acting like kids. Isn't that how they are supposed to act?

The editors of the *United Methodist Reporter* suggested in a collectively written January 1991 column that cliches about young people are too often accepted as conventional wisdom or gospel truth. How true! "Those kids don't have a serious bone in their bodies," "Church membership means nothing to kids these days," and "All kids today are selfish," are, like all other such statements, unfair generalizations.

When my friend Judy and I were teenagers, we were asked

to sing a duet during the morning worship service at our church. We practiced several times before our debut and sounded quite good.

But when Sunday arrived, the butterflies in our stomachs did, too. We walked sedately to the platform after the pastor announced our song, but when the pianist played the introduction, all that came out of our mouths was laughter.

Has something ever struck you so funny that, no matter how hard you tried, you couldn't stop giggling? That's what happened to us that morning. I can just imagine what the adults were thinking: *Those girls are so silly; will they ever grow up? Don't they have any respect for God's house?* Our parents almost died of embarrassment.

But Judy and I *did* grow up and, with Christian husbands at our sides, raised our children to know and love our Lord.

Unfortunately, too many of us grown-ups have forgotten what we were like at various stages along the way. We grew up—and our kids will, too. What we need is patience. Individuals mature at different rates physically, mentally, emotionally, and spiritually. We must allow them the time they need and trust that it will be according to God's perfect schedule for them.

In an appearance before a large audience of adults at Chautauqua Institution, Chautauqua, New York, in June 1987, Fred Rogers of "Mister Rogers' Neighborhood" fame shared one of his secrets for relating to children:

"I try," he said in his modest, deliberate way, "to keep open the pathway to my own childhood."

What profound advice for parents! If we can remember how *we* felt as children and teenagers, it is so much easier to communicate our love and respect to our youngsters. And when our own love for God is the basis of that open communication, love, and respect, our children will learn that they can trust Him, as well.

Questions for Thought

1. What are some concrete ways I can improve my listening skills? Toward God? Toward my mate? Toward my children?

2. When have I felt most successful in communicating with my children? What can I learn from those experiences?

3. How can I better model good manners in everyday living situations?

4. Can I recall a humorous—or not-so-humorous—experience in our family caused by a missed signal or a misunderstanding?

5

Making God Real Through Fun Days and Sundays

Children love the rituals and hoopla that surround holidays, birthdays, or any family time. While some youngsters find the extra people, special foods, later bedtimes, and general excitement overstimulating, most relish a change from the normal routine and enjoy calendar countdowns to such red-letter days.

Given the hectic pace of our lives and the difficulties we adults face in choosing good, better, and best commitments of our time, we sometimes sigh over the extra work required by the holiday and fun-time happenings children hold so dear. But helping our children to build good memories into the foundations of their lives is an essential part of our job description as parents.

Perhaps you can dig your way back in your memory to family reunions you did not want to attend but ended up enjoying immensely. Or maybe, like me, you recall big Sunday dinners complete with roast beef, mashed potatoes, gravy, and Mom's best apple pie. (I remember the dishes, too, all done by hand. Yet Grandma and I had some great talks over the kitchen sink!)

Traditions, Traditions . . .

A friend of mine shared the details of a recent event she knows her children will always remember. For her father-in-law's seventieth birthday, all five of his grown children, each of their spouses, and all ten grandchildren arrived at Grandpa's for a slumber party! The first to get tired got the beds. Each of the rest found a spot on the floor. The whole family enjoyed the celebration so much it would not surprise me if it became a yearly tradition!

It is important to establish traditions in our families. Some will involve grandmas, grandpas, aunts, uncles, cousins, and maybe even family friends; others will be just for Mom, Dad, brothers, and sisters. And some will revolve around time spent with individual family members, one-on-one.

The memories of wonderful times spent with those who love and care about us can be a source of personal strength and joy for parents and kids alike when difficult times come. And sharing them with our own mates and children helps us pass on:

1. glimpses of life when we were small
2. insight into values we hold dear
3. the priceless heritage of family jokes and fun
4. a sense of closeness

When my husband, Wes, was little, his grandpa was the Sunday school superintendent at the church Wes's family attended. Grandpa Chall always had Hershey's Kisses in his suit pocket on Sunday mornings, and when the children saw him coming, they ran to reach into his pocket for their weekly treat—"Silver Tops!" Wes remembers saying proudly one day to a friend, "That's *my* grandpa."

Guess what sweet was often found in the candy jar when our children were growing up? You're right—Hershey's Kisses! And guess what Wes puts in his pockets every time he visits his grandchildren? Right again! And he's a dentist!

Special! Special! Special!—Family Fun Times

Developing family traditions and including fun days in our families' lives need not be expensive or elaborate. But regularity is important in offering our children the security and solid undergirding of numerous together times. With today's busy agendas, many families find that unless such events are written on the kitchen calendar (and Dad's and Mom's pocket planners, too), they just won't happen. Some families find it helpful to set aside one night a week as a family night. Yes, children need to know the value of work, obligations, and flexibility, but in the area of family together times, too many disappointments and broken promises tell children, "You don't matter."

Here are some ideas to adapt or adopt with your children:

1. Popcorn at the movies—Rent a family video. Make popcorn and provide iced juices or soft drinks. If your children are small, they might like to buy their treats with nickels and dimes earned during the day performing extra chores. Playing store is fun; it allows them to help you, and they will understand the value of money a bit better. Cozy up in your favorite chairs or stretch out on the floor to relax and enjoy.

2. Family theater talent shows—After a short rehearsal, let the kids put on a play or stage a talent show for their parents and/or relatives. Suggest that they sell handmade tickets at the door. (Perhaps the proceeds could go to a favorite charity or toward another family together-time project.) If the weather cooperates, hold the event outdoors, stringing clotheslines and draping blankets to create a stage. Be sure to express your appreciation with applause; curtain calls are in order. If you are invited to participate, be a good sport. Ham it up and revel in your children's delighted surprise!

3. Family roundtable—Set aside an occasional dinner-time, as your children get older, to discuss current issues and events, abortion, war, dating, world politics, prophecy, Christ's return, in the light of Scripture. It's a great way to get to know what your child is thinking. You may need to do a bit of studying beforehand; your pastor and local Christian bookstore owner are good resource people.

Don't be afraid of children's honest, sometimes difficult questions. It is always appropriate to say, "I don't know, but I can find out"; they will respect your honesty. And don't worry or be shocked when *they* express such candid fears or feelings as, in the case of a discussion of Christ's Second Coming, "I hope I can go to college, get married, and have a baby before Jesus comes back." That's a natural reaction and part of the maturing process. Reminding youngsters of such biblical characters as the apostle Paul, who thought Jesus might come back in *his* lifetime, and Jesus Himself, who said even *He* didn't know the day or hour of His return (Matthew 24:36), offers them a different perspective and the realization that they are dealing with age-old issues Christians down through the centuries also struggled to understand.

4. Nature walks—Even two-year-olds enjoy short walks in the woods, along a beach, or to the park. (Backpacks or strollers can make the difference between fun and frustration.) Give each child a brown paper lunch bag or a small plastic bowl and ask him or her to find things God has made or things that tell us spring (or fall, summer, or winter) is coming. Walk slowly. Let your little ones watch birds hopping on the lawn or digging for worms. Turn over a rock and see what is underneath. Feel the moss on the trees. What a perfect time to praise God out loud for all He has created for us to enjoy!

5. Christian music fests—Enormous Christian music festivals have sprung up all over the country, and they are great opportunities for family vacations, especially as your children hit the teen years. Check with your local Christian bookstore for information.

You can create your *own* Christian music fests by teaching your children to enjoy all kinds of religious music very early in their lives. Christian bookstores carry many wonderful, spiritually enriching music tapes for children and adults. Install a cassette deck in your car, or remember to take along a small portable player, and turn routine trips into family sing-alongs.

As your children get older, be sensitive: Don't force *your* musical choices on them. Try to provide contemporary Christian music, if possible, that is relevant to their ages and musical preferences. For further discussion of this topic, *see* Chapter 6, "Tackling Those Tough Problems."

6. Cooking classes—Where do children like to play? Right under Mom's feet in the kitchen! Kids love to cook. Let them dump and stir. Be brave enough to let them pour. (Just be sure the containers from which they are pouring are only partially full.)

As children get older, they enjoy having their own dough to shape into piecrust pastries or cookies while you finish your part of the baking. A mini-cookbook is included at the end of this book. It contains not only recipes for goodies you and your child can make together but also some conversation starters and other ideas for using cooking classes to enhance your child's understanding of God and the Christian life.

Remember Emily? She and others like her have learned that even little children can:

- scrub vegetables
- shape meatballs
- wash fruit
- wash, dry, and put away nonbreakable dishes
- arrange foodstuffs on cupboard shelves
- wipe tables and mop floors

But make these jobs part of the fun of being together. Kitchen activities lend themselves beautifully to comments concerning God's provisions for us and your child's ability and willingness to be a helper.

7. One-on-one times—Some of the above activities can be adapted to high-quality one-on-one times, when Mom or Dad spends time with an individual child doing something that pleases them both or that teaches a necessary household or mechanical skill and provides some togetherness. One-on-one times need to start early in a child's life if parent-child relationships are to mature in preparation for the busy, stressful years of adolescence.

If the budget allows, it is fun to schedule lunch dates for dad and daughter or mother and son. Private shopping trips (without little brothers and sisters) and a stop at the Tastee Freeze for ice cream are another alternative. Regular walks, bicycle rides, ball games—or whatever parent and child like to do with each other—foster the relaxed atmosphere that encourages trust and exchanged confidences.

As is the case with all types of family fun, one-on-one times need to be regular, expected events in a child's life. Betsey's story shows us why.

Betsey was one of my preschool students, and her aggressive behavior in recent weeks had been earning her lots of my attention—negative (albeit kind) attention. Her mother, Susan, made an appointment to talk with me about her daughter's actions.

Somewhere in the course of our conversation, I asked if Susan and her husband regularly made time to spend just with Betsey. Susan burst into tears and explained that she and Betsey's daddy had been extremely busy lately with their son, Michael, who had developed severe asthma and needed frequent visits to a major hospital in a nearby city. In the family's concern over Michael, their usual rituals with Betsey, among them her afternoon story time, had been forgotten.

When I saw Susan a couple of days later, she reported that she and Betsey had taken a grocery shopping trip together. "I can't believe what one shopping trip did!" she exclaimed. Her mother's exclusive time and attention and the importance of being Mom's big helper had already made a difference in Betsey's self-esteem, and her behavior improved rapidly.

8. Family vacations—Do you like to rough it in a tent? Backpack along the Appalachian Trail? Does your family prefer to go the Holiday Inn route? Or do you do a little of both, with a recreational vehicle in tow?

Do your work schedule and budget allow for two-week holiday trips? Or do three-day weekends or occasional day trips fit your lifestyle better?

How we take family vacations does not matter. Fancy or plain, long or short, what counts is that we plan for family vacations on the calendar and in the bank account—and that we follow through if at all possible. If we cave in to the pressures of everyday living ("I just *can't* get away from the office!"), we'll wake up someday and look back with regret at missed opportunities for family closeness.

Perhaps your family will choose to spend all or part of one vacation with the extended family. It will be time well invested, enriching children's sense of their heritage and permitting them to interact with people of differing ages, personalities, and lifestyles.

Time spent with the primary family alone is vital, also, and renews Mom, Dad, brothers, and sisters for a return to the daily grind. And if possible, longer vacations need to include or be specifically structured around some one-on-one time—Mom with Dad, Dad with Sis, Mom with little brother, and so on.

I remember one vacation when the Lemans and Challs combined time for all of the above-mentioned emphases. Gathering at Lake Tahoe with extended-family members, we opted to make mealtimes as simple as possible by placing everyone's name in a hat—kids included. Teams were then assigned meals, and each did the planning, shopping, preparation, and cleanup. Fifteen years later, one of our kids still talks about being on Uncle Jack's team!

The together time was great, but so were the walks along the beach with my brother Jack, shopping with Sande and Linda, sitting quietly to reminisce with my dad, and playing games with the children. Without taking the time for quiet moments during vacation, things could have become hectic, with no time to get past the small talk and down to the nitty-gritty of sharing thoughts and feelings.

Birthdays Are the Greatest!

In our home birthdays were always special. Karin, Kristine, and Tom each were allowed to choose their favorite meal on their day. Guess what all three of them always picked? Turkey—with all the trimmings! It took a lot of time and effort to put those dinners together, especially for the birthday that invariably seemed to occur on one of July's hottest days, but I didn't mind.

Our children enjoyed the usual kid-style parties, but we celebrated with our extended family, as well. It was great to have Grandma, Grandpa, Aunt Cindy, Uncle Dick, and cousin Kirsten come to help light the candles and sing "Happy Birthday." We always added a chorus, to the same tune, that went like this:

> God bless you today,
> God bless you always.
> God bless you and keep you,
> Another year through.

We wanted God to be a guest at our celebrations. And Dad's prayer, making special mention of the birthday boy or girl and the family's thankfulness for his or her presence in our lives, was strong reinforcement of our Christian family values.

I recall cutting the first piece of my birthday cake when I was a little girl and making the traditional secret, don't-tell-anyone, once-a-year wish. With each passing celebration it never changed: I wanted to love and serve God always.

An abnormal wish for a young child, perhaps? What about longings for dolls and bikes and fabulous vacations? Well, my Christian mother had made God real in my life. Even as a child I knew that I loved Jesus and He loved me.

Why do I share this? To remind you that we never know when God is quietly at work deep down in the lives of our children. Birthdays can be times for reflection, for joy, for goal-setting. Make the most of their potential for reaffirming God's love and your love for your family members!

Through the Year: Holiday Fun Can Make God Real, Too

Let's look now at how we can use holiday rituals to create wonderful family memories and make God real to our children at the same time.

Valentine's Day.

February 14 is traditionally a day for lovers to celebrate the joys of friendship and romance. As such it is an ideal opportunity to let your children glimpse the love you share with your mate and the wonderful benefits of Christian marriage. If you are a single parent, use this holiday to rejoice in friendships within the family and outside it, too.

Encourage your kids to make valentines for each parent, and for grandpas and grandmas, as well. Or make a batch of heart-shaped cookies, decorate them together, and share with family members, friends, or perhaps a lonely shut-in who won't get much attention on this holiday.

If you are shopping for a card, gift, or both for your mate, let your little ones in on the surprise, if you think they can handle the suspense! And if you are planning an evening out with your date, take time to share with your children the importance of mommies and daddies making the effort to enrich their friendship and love. This is a great time to emphasize friendship in general and to liken the time we spend in developing human relationships to the time we need to spend in deepening our relationship with God.

Easter.

What time of year could be more perfect for sharing with our children the joy of eternal life than Easter? Yet the events of the first Easter can boggle the minds of adults. How do we explain them to children?

Here are a few suggestions:

1. Check with your local Christian bookstore for child-oriented books containing the Easter story. One that our family liked was *The Story of Easter for Children*, published by Ideals Publishing Corporation, Nashville, Tennessee. Beautifully illustrated and simply told in verse, it seemed to tie everything together so that little ones could understand.

2. Last year at our family Easter dinner gathering, each person found a plastic egg at his or her place. Inside was a small slip of paper with a verse of Scripture highlighting one part of the Easter story. The papers were numbered one to ten, and we read them in turn. Prayer time followed.

Those family members who couldn't read found picture messages such as these: I (picture of an eye) LOVE (picture of a heart) JESUS (picture of Jesus), and JESUS (picture of

Jesus) A-ROSE (picture of a rose). Each family member could share in the joy of Christ's resurrection.

For dessert that day we served cut-out sugar cookies shaped like crosses.

3. Easter caroling does sound rather unusual, but wouldn't it be fun? Why not take your family or a group of families from church and sing triumphant Easter hymns for some shut-ins or nursing-home patients? Add some Easter candies and cookies for a middle-of-the-year treat. You will be sharing the joy of Christ's resurrection with the caregivers, too.

4. Have you given up sending Christmas cards? How about sending Easter greetings—even a few—to faraway grandparents or to shut-ins? Let your children help to select cards, taking time to discuss the real meaning of Easter. Better yet, let them design their own cards. Give them paper, markers, crayons, stickers, and/or pastel tempera paint and some appropriately shaped cookie cutters for printing. If you have explained that Easter means more than new clothes and candy-filled baskets and that you hope their cards will share the Easter message, you may be surprised and delighted with your children's attempts to represent the Easter chronicle.

A parish worker tells of sharing the Easter story with her congregation of junior worshipers. She is one of those teachers who makes stories live, and the children love her. At the end of this particular lesson, she explained to the boys and girls that Jesus would be coming back again.

"I can hardly wait," shouted four-year-old Kris, jumping up from her chair in the first row.

We expect children to be excited about new toys or trips to the zoo, but to see them excited about Jesus is super!

Thanksgiving.

If I were to ask a group of three-year-olds to tell me some things they were thankful for, I doubt if I would get much response. They would probably give me a blank stare. But if I rephrased the question and asked them to tell me what makes them happy, they would produce quite a list.

Teacher: "Who can think of something that makes you happy?"

Child: "I got a new toy."

Teacher: "Great! Jimmy is thankful for his new toy. Who has a cozy bed to sleep in?"

Children: "I do!" "I have a big bed!" "Me, me, me!" "My teddy bear sleeps with me!"

Teacher: "I bet you're all thankful for your nice, warm beds. Thank you, God, for beds to sleep in."

The same type of scenario can happen at home. One family I know uses thank-you prayers around the dining room table, at story time, or just before bed.

In another home, each person in the family takes a turn writing a short thank-you note and leaving it under the dinner plate of the person for whom it is intended. Small children will need help in preparing theirs. Other families write Thanksgiving-oriented Scripture verses on colored construction-paper leaves. They make lovely place cards and can be read before the mealtime prayer on Thanksgiving Day.

Still another young mom sits down with her children and thumbs through a stack of old magazines to find pictures depicting the things for which they are most thankful. Then everyone pitches in to cut out and paste their choices on a large piece of poster board or brown wrapping paper (taped temporarily to the floor for convenience) that bears the heading "WE THANK GOD FOR. . . ." The resulting masterpiece is hung on the family room wall.

Christmas.

We all know it is easy to get children hyped up about Santa Claus, presents, tree trimming, and Christmas cookies, but how do we communicate the real meaning of Christmas? How can parents prevent the best Christmas gift of all—Jesus—from being lost amid the toys and tinsel?

If receiving God's most precious gift, His only Son, is to be the focus of your family's Christmas celebrations, try putting some of the following ideas into practice:

1. Gift giving. By planning ahead, you can use the Christmas season as a springboard to get your family involved in sharing the spirit of Christmas all year long. Since talk of God and His gifts to us is a natural by-product of any discussion about presents, start early in the year (even during the cold, cabin fever days of January) to work on those neat ideas you always read about on December 15. As you enjoy sharing the anticipation of a loved one's pleasure in some special item, conversations about our Lord and His concern for our welfare and happiness may arise as a matter of course.

Creative gift giving can incorporate seven qualities that teach important values to youngsters:

1. It can be fun.
2. It can be tailored to the receiver's needs and interests.
3. It need not be expensive.
4. It may be done anonymously.
5. It is an expression of our love in Christ for others.

6. It can encourage or uplift the receiver.
7. It expects nothing in return.

The list of possibilities for child-made gifts is endless. Let children:

- help make breads, cookies, and candies
- decorate food gift containers with Con-Tact paper and permanent markers
- paint pictures
- design ornaments (Picture ornaments make wonderful keepsakes.)
- print wrapping paper and gift bags with cookie cutters, stencils, or cross sections of fruit dipped in paint
- wrap presents (Kids love cellophane tape!)
- create objects from homemade modeling dough
- help root plant cuttings, pot them, and decorate the containers
- make "Play Clay" for friends (*see* mini-cookbook, page 189). Be sure to give in airtight containers.
- make greeting cards
- save some of their allowance in a specially decorated jar to give to the needy at Christmas
- make cassette tapes for grandparents

2. Advent calendars. Elegantly crafted or simply designed, handmade or store-bought, advent calendars help children keep track of how long they must wait for Jesus' birthday. Pick a special time each day to peek behind the door. If you choose calendars with a Christian theme, you can take advantage of each tiny picture or object to initiate Christmas conversations with your little ones.

3. The Advent wreath. Used as a centerpiece on the dining room table or elsewhere in your home, the Advent wreath symbolizes the coming of Jesus as the Light of the world. Make your own wreath, or buy one if crafts are not your strong point. Many small pamphlets, some especially designed for family use, are available at Christian bookstores to help you understand and interpret the Christmas story through the lighting of each of four candles, one each Sunday for the four weeks preceding Christmas.

The ceremony of lighting the Advent wreath together may motivate family brainstorming sessions on the meaning of our Christian faith, on the needs of others, or on the words of Scripture. With Mom's and Dad's help, children can take turns lighting the candles each Sunday. (This process alone will probably yield some opportunities to discuss sharing!) Excitement will build as each week draws the family closer to Jesus' birthday celebration.

4. A manger scene purchased for your home is not a luxury but a wise investment in the process of making God real to your children. Forget the porcelain, "don't touch" varieties of crèches. Save those for when the children are older. Many attractive, unbreakable sets are available in every price range. Perhaps for budgetary reasons you will choose to purchase Mary, Joseph, and the Baby Jesus one Christmas and add animals, angels, shepherds, and wise men a few at a time in succeeding years. Include the children in such shopping trips, and let them help select the figures. As you unpack and set up the scene, retell the Christmas story; handling the tiny figures makes that long-ago event become very real.

Some families allow each child to have a manger scene in his or her room, perhaps purchased by grandparents and intended to go with the child when he or she leaves home. And in some homes it is customary for the parents to place the Baby Jesus in each separate manger after the children go to sleep on Christmas Eve. When they awake on Christmas morning, Baby Jesus is lying there. He is born!

5. Tree-trimming parties can be precious primary family events, but there is no reason grandparents or friends can't be invited to join in the fun. Put on Christmas music and sing together as you carefully unwrap the ornaments and hang them on the tree. Children love the tradition of seeing the familiar ornaments reappear each year, and they like to add new ornaments, too.

There is an extraspecial ornament in our Christmas box, presented to me by our daughter Kristine when she was a small girl. Made of paper and decorated in pencil and crayon, it depicts the Baby Jesus in a tiny manger. Amid the crayoned straw is a small slit, enabling the Baby Jesus to be picked up and loved. In His hand is a rattle, and at the top of the ornament Kristine wrote, "HE IS BORN!"

I think the coming of the Baby Jesus was real to Kristine, don't you?

Here is some food for thought—and it may not be easy to swallow. Consider giving up your dreams of the perfectly decorated tree and house while your children are small. What is more important, a tree that looks like you won a magazine's "Country Christmas" contest, or a tree your children can point to with a sense of accomplishment? Believe me, there will be plenty of years for placing your home on the local house and garden club's Christmas tour. But your children's interest in preparing for the holidays will wane all too soon. Enjoy it while you can, and remember that their self-esteem is fragile.

Do not reject their creative efforts to decorate; instead, try to understand what they can do at their ages and encourage them to participate.

6. Christmas at church. Take advantage of your church's Christmas programming to make God real to your family during this wonderful season. Helping to decorate the sanctuary, singing carols, giving to the Christmas offering, and participating in the Sunday school pageant can offer many opportunities to share the Christmas message with children. But be careful: Plan your schedule so that church activities are not crammed in at the last minute or treated as "oughts" instead of "want tos." Children pick up on our moods easily, and if they sense that we feel too rushed, busy, or frazzled to enter joyfully into what is going on in our church home, they will project their own resentment at our bad attitudes on to the church—and on to God.

7. Christmas Day. Several suggestions gleaned from various families can enrich our celebrations on Christmas morning.

For some families, Christmas Eve or Christmas morning church services are established traditions. Again, remember to plan meals and travel time carefully so as to leave plenty of relaxed time for such events. Racing into a Christmas service with a disgruntled, hurried family does little for anyone's spiritual enrichment!

One family I know celebrates the Christ Child's birth by holding hands on Christmas morning in front of the brightly lit tree, before the presents are opened. Dad prays, and everyone sings "O Christmas Tree."

Other families take time to read, tell, or act out the Christmas story, both before and on Christmas Day. Admittedly, long, drawn-out rituals try the patience of kids who are anxious to open gifts, so don't alienate them by bearing down or preaching at this point. But kept brief and simple, acknowledgment that this is *Jesus'* birthday puts gift giving and receiving in perspective.

A birthday cake for Jesus can be the perfect dessert for Christmas dinner. Buy one at the bakery or make it at home together, involving your children in this act of love. Top your favorite cake with white icing, red and green trim, a manger scene, or "Happy Birthday, Jesus." Be sure to sing, "Happy Birthday, Jesus" before you cut the cake. The children will be happy to act on His behalf by blowing out the candles! We have already noted that kids love birthdays, and this simple expression of our love for Him can make a big impression.

One last thought: As you enjoy the Christmas story together throughout the year and throughout the season, make sure your children understand that Jesus is not a baby any longer. He grew bigger and bigger; He played with His friends; He helped His family; He loved to worship God in the temple. And as a grown-up, He had a big job to do—telling people about God and about heaven.

Sundays Can Be Fun Days, Too

Which of the following describes the atmosphere at your house on Sunday morning?

Hide and Seek: "Where *are* your Sunday shoes?"

Penny Hunt: "Put your offering in your pocket and leave it there. You're going to lose it!"

Red Rover, Red Rover, Dare You to Come Over: "Mommy, Tom's being mean to me!"

Red Light, Green Light: "Hurry up and eat your breakfast. We're going to be late!"

Tag: "Stop running around this minute! Sit on the sofa and stay clean while we finish getting ready."

Or do your Sunday mornings usually run smoothly?

"Ready, everyone? Wow, we're right on time this morning, dinner is in the oven, and each of you looks so nice!"

Don't worry if that last scenario seems to elude you: you are not alone. I think the Sunday Morning Syndrome, as I like to call it, is a reality for most of us. And Satan delights in encouraging it, seemingly working overtime to create chaos in Christian homes on the Lord's Day.

Why does it seem much easier to get ourselves moving every other day of the week?

Part of the problem could be that on Sunday we are all getting ready to leave at once, which is not our normal weekday pattern. And on Sundays we want to sleep in a bit longer, enjoy a leisurely breakfast, watch TV, read the morning paper, and get the noon meal under way. It is hard to do all of that and still have a family of four, five, or six (plus?) ready to leave for Sunday school by 9:20 A.M.!

What Can Parents Do to Turn Sunday Into a Fun Day?

Preparation is the key for parents who wish to banish the Sunday Morning Syndrome. And preparation takes (here it comes again!) parental self-discipline. But what can you lose? Try these simple steps for four weeks and watch Sundays become fun days at your house.

During the week:

1. Study your Sunday school lesson, and encourage the children to study theirs, or review the previous week's

take-home papers with them. (Be sure to read any notes from Sunday school teachers; they may contain great ideas for applying the Sunday school lesson at home.) This activity could be part of a together time, accompanied by snacks and replacing a half hour or an hour of television.

On Saturday:

1. Fill the gas tank.
2. Iron and lay out Sunday clothing. (And have the children locate their shoes!)
3. Take baths, wash hair.
4. Plan simple Sunday meals, doing as much preparation as possible to minimize cooking and cleanup on the Lord's Day.
5. Set the table for Sunday morning breakfast or dinner.
6. If possible, make plans to spend Sunday afternoon in pursuits that rest and refresh family members—visiting friends or relatives, reading good books, playing games, napping, walking. (For an excellent, biblical look at the kind of rest God intends for us to enjoy on Sundays, read Gordon MacDonald's book *Ordering Your Private World* [Thomas Nelson Publishers, 1985].)
7. Get to bed at a reasonable hour.

On Sunday morning:

1. Get up at a reasonable hour.
2. Use Christian music as a wake-up call for everyone and to help your family prepare for worship. (If your

car has a tape deck, continue listening during the ride to church.)

3. Share household chores. Kids can load the dishwasher or help fix a salad while Mom finishes her hair and makeup.

4. Once at church, enter wholeheartedly into Sunday school and worship activities and into opportunities for fellowship with other Christians. When children see their parents participating joyously, the attitude rubs off on them. And it's more likely to stick for a lifetime!

5. If going out for dinner after church is on the agenda, parents should either decide on a restaurant privately or allow family members to take turns week by week.

Let me add one final thought as we consider how to make Sundays fun days. What about those children whose families don't—or won't—take them to church? Inviting them to share in our family fun also takes some advance planning, but it teaches our kids the joy of hospitality. And the rewards can be eternal.

Craig's mom and dad, for instance, were not interested in church, but his aunt, a widow with three children of her own, took him to Sunday school and morning worship each week and saw to it that he attended youth group and junior choir. Somehow she always made Craig feel that including him was no trouble at all.

Craig looked forward to those Sunday rituals and grew to love the Lord. Today he is on the mission field, thanks to an aunt who cared, a God who reached down to him, and a congregation of fellow Christians who supported him all the way.

*   *   *

Taking the steps we've mentioned is so simple, yet so hard. Once we learn to incorporate them into our weekend plans, however, they become habit. And the results—peaceful, enjoyable, fun-day Sundays—are so satisfying!

Remember, fun days and Sundays need not be big events; it is more important for them to be a regular, expected part of life in your home. That kind of routine lays a solid foundation of happy memories on which your children can build their lives.

Questions for Thought

1. What are some meaningful traditions in our family?

2. How faithful am I in scheduling family together times— and in following through on our plans?

3. What specific actions can I take this year to use holidays and other fun days to make God real to my children?

4. Is Sunday a fun day at our house? If not, what steps can I take to make it one?

6

Tackling Those Tough
Problems

Certain issues seem to be common denominators in the
child-rearing process. Most parents and children will strug-
gle over one or more of them along the way. In this chapter
we will look at ten tough problems and discuss some strategies for reaching acceptable parent-child guidelines and/or
compromises.

1. "I'm a Little Scared"—Dealing With Children's Fears

It is very normal for young children to become fearful at
times. It's a big world out there, and children have so many
firsts to encounter. Fred Rogers's comment about keeping
open the pathways to our childhood certainly applies here.
We adults have so many experiences and so much knowledge
to draw on, and it is easy to forget how it felt to face a social
setting, academic challenge, or daily living task for the very
first time.

A little boy who had expressed fears about entering the first grade was asked why.

"Because I don't know what they're going to teach me when I get there," he replied.

It would be tempting for any adult to say, "Of course you don't! That's why you need to go." But the child's answer epitomizes the way little ones feel as they confront new experiences. A large percentage of childhood fears arise simply from the fact of not knowing.

One measure we can take in dealing with fears, then, is to prevent them by preparing our children when we know they will be treading on new turf. Be careful: Such prevention must be done in a casual, relaxed manner so as not to introduce more grounds for fear by overemphasizing the uncertainties of a first-time experience. Still, taking a child step-by-step through an upcoming situation mentally (and physically, if possible and desirable), gearing our explanations and language to his or her age and maturity, asking questions to be sure he or she understands, and repeating the process, if necessary, can ensure fewer surprises and better adaptation to unfamiliar events, surroundings, and people.

Here's how it works:

"Johnny, you know we're meeting the whole family at a lovely restaurant tomorrow night to celebrate Aunt Shirley and Uncle Bob's anniversary. Let's talk for a minute about what it will be like. First we'll have an early lunch so we can get our nap over with and have time to get dressed. What will you wear? Let's look in your closet and choose two outfits. Then you can pick out the one in which you'll be most comfortable. Yes, your cousins will be there, too. In fact, you'll know almost everyone at this party, but if there are some people you don't know, all you need to do is smile; you don't need to talk unless you want to. No, you won't be able to ride in the front seat with Daddy on the way; he has to go early to get some surprises ready for Aunt Shirley and Uncle Bob. But we'll ride with Uncle Jim, and we can sit with Daddy at the dinner table. . . ."

This step-by-step approach can help us prepare our children for new baby-sitters, thunderstorms, visits to the doctor, stays in the hospital, weddings or funerals (if it seems wise to take your child, depending on his or her age and closeness to the people involved),* toilet training, plane or train rides, church events, or long trips in the car. In fact, we do our children a disservice if we fail to prepare them. Too many fears are born when we allow our youngsters to fumble into situations for which they are not ready.

When a child is afraid because circumstances have thrust him or her into something new or hurtful before we have been able to offer explanations, we need to acknowledge the validity of his or her feelings.

"Yes, Sharon, I can understand how frightened you must have felt when the dog came running at you barking. I would have been scared, too." Never disparage a child's feelings or make him or her feel silly for having expressed them.

Here again Christian parents have wonderful opportunities to make God real to our children, for we have the resources available to help alleviate their fears. After letting a youngster release his or her feelings and acknowledging that they are normal and valid, gently and lovingly share the truths from the Bible about God's love, protection, and power. Then pray with your child about the situation. It may be necessary to repeat

---

* *See* chapter 7 for further discussion of fears about death, illness, separation, going to heaven, and so on.

this process several times, depending on the child's age and the severity of the fright. But relief should come eventually. If it doesn't, consider asking a trusted pastor to talk with the child or to recommend another professional who can help.

2. "I Can't Make Up My Mind!"—Helping Kids Make Choices

It is important for parents to realize that almost every issue we help our children face as youngsters is a prototype of some issue they will face as adults.

Making choices is a good example of this principle. Clothing styles, schedule conflicts, and, "Which stuffed animal shall I take to bed tonight?" may not seem like life-and-death matters to us. But the very process of learning to make those decisions, and to live with the consequences, prepares our kids for choices they will have to make in the future. And some of *those* choices—of mates, careers, and, most important, whether or not to yield their lives to God—*will* be vital to their happiness on earth and in heaven.

The key to teaching your children how to make choices *they* can live with lies in allowing them to make choices within limits—limits *you* can live with. You might, for example, say, "Ben, which of these two outfits would you like to wear to Sunday school today?" If you have already selected two suitable sets of clothes, it doesn't really matter which he decides on, but he feels keenly the freedom of choice.

Or perhaps Katie is getting ready for school and you want to help. "Katie, I could do your hair in a ponytail, two pigtails, or with a hair band today. Which will it be?" Do not say, "How do you want me to fix your hair?" Too many choices not only confuse the child, they can box you into a corner.

"I'd like it in a French braid, please, Mom."

"I don't know how to do a French braid, Katie."

"Well, you *asked* how I wanted you to fix it!"

The strategy of offering choices within limits is particularly helpful when kids hit the joining years and every club, sport, and committee invites their participation. Discuss with your mate what your values, budget, and schedule will tolerate, and then allow a child to choose one, two, or three out of five or six acceptable activities.

Some youngsters inevitably agonize and seesaw even over limited choices. But in narrowing the possibilities, you have enabled them to center on the decision-making process itself, a necessary adult skill. Let them whine and fuss briefly, but be firm in your limits and in setting a time frame, if necessary, for making a final choice.

Sometimes in life we do not have choices. If your child's preschool requires that gym shoes be worn to class for safety reasons, then four-year-old Susan cannot wear her black patent leather sandals. And if Jack's school basketball training rules state that he is to be in bed by 11:00 P.M., he cannot stay at the school carnival past 10:30. Helping children to understand that some things are nonnegotiable is part of our job as parents. And seeing our firm but loving limits will help them when they stand face-to-face with the (for-our-own-good) requirements of a just but loving God.

3. "Jane Who?"—Friends, Friends, Friends

Do we know our children's friends? Do they know us? Do we know something about their parents and their home lives?

Do we see those parents socially or at church and community functions?

The best insurance against detrimental peer influences when children are older is to provide them with plenty of friends early in life whose parents and lifestyles we identify with and with whom we like to spend time. Here, again, our Christian faith and church involvement can help by providing a network of families with similar values.

When fourteen-year-old Linnea's dad died, Linnea and her mom already had a close relationship, which helped them both through the next three years. But when Linnea was a high school senior she began to assert her independence, insisting on traveling fifteen hundred miles south with her friends over Easter break.

Linnea's mom panicked for a few days, but then she began to pray. Since she knew the parents of the girls involved, she called a meeting to discuss the big vacation. Together the families made a commitment to go south as a group and stay in the same motel complex. At first the girls were slightly disappointed at the prospect of adult supervision, but the compromise worked, and everyone had a great time. Linnea's mother was lucky to have known those parents.

Knowing our children's friends' families helps in other situations, too. While not all Christian families will see eye-to-eye on setting comparable teenage ground rules, it is worth discussing. And when a child comes home with, "Mom, I'm the only one who has to come home early," or "Dad, everybody is going," it is nice to be able to check things out with other parents.

One more advantage of knowing our children's friends and their parents is the ability to pray for them—and to know they pray for us. The Book of Ecclesiastes says, "Two are better than one" (4:9 NIV), and Jesus said that if two of us agree about anything we ask that fits in with His best plan for us, God will answer our prayer (*see* Matthew 18:19; James 4:2, 3). Joining forces in prayer for one another's children is one of the best gifts we Christians can offer our brothers and sisters in the faith. And if we let our children know that we and others are praying for specific needs in their lives and rejoice with them when our prayers are answered, the awareness of God's power and intervention will build their faith in His reality.

This sounds great, you say, but what if there are no youngsters our children's age at our church? And what if our kids choose friends, later on, of whom we disapprove?

If you discover early in your child-rearing years that the church you attend has few or no children for yours to be friends with, you may have to assess carefully the impact that will have on them as time goes on. If changing churches is not an option, perhaps you can enroll your youngsters in a children's ministry or youth group offered on Sunday nights or midweek by another congregation. Getting involved with a second church family has its complications and can stretch you both timewise and emotionally, but it may be worth doing for the sake of your kids. And God may work through the circumstances to bless you in unexpected ways!

We can only hope and pray that our children will develop Christian values at an early age so that they will choose appropriate friends as they approach the impressionable junior high and high school years. If they do not, make a point of getting to know the friends they do choose. Make your children's friends welcome in your home, and find out as much as possible about their backgrounds. With loving prayer and supervision, you and your family may end up influencing them!

4. "Turn That Radio Down!"—The Music Dilemma

In chapter 5 we discussed the boost that Christian music can give to our efforts to make God real to our children. While few Christian parents have problems relating to modern, upbeat versions of children's Sunday school songs, the advent of rock music—even *Christian* rock music—for teens is of concern to many.

Gospel singer Sandi Patti addressed this dilemma in a 1989 interview with free-lance writer Christine Willett Greenwald. She pointed out that Jesus used different methods to reach different people, talking to fishermen in terms they could understand but reaching tax collectors and persons from other walks of life with parables and stories tailored to their comprehension. She acknowledged freely that she did not expect teenagers to flock to her concerts, but she said that Christian teens do need an alternative to the secular music around which so much of their culture revolves. She suggested that before parents condemn Christian rock music along with its secular counterpart, they should investigate Christian music artists individually, listening to their music and requesting articles about them and their world views from reliable magazines such as *Christian Contemporary Music* or *Campus Life*.

Once we have satisfied ourselves that certain artists are portraying Christian values, we may need to be tolerant, if not thrilled, about our children's choices of music. Receptivity to their kind of music may hurt our ears temporarily, but it will go a long way toward demonstrating God's unconditional love and our willingness to meet them where they are.

I am not saying we parents have to listen to music or allow our youngsters to listen to music that flaunts the world's perversions and belittles our Christian values. We do have the right to disallow music we find offensive in content. But if our approach toward this delicate subject demonstrates love, honesty, and openness, we may find ourselves in the midst of some productive discussions about the mindsets and values represented by our kids' musical favorites.

One of my friends told her eleven-year-old son, who was just beginning to discover boomboxes, headphones, and teen culture in general, "I don't mind lively music as long as the lyrics are clean and decent." She began purchasing Christian contemporary and Christian rock music tapes, many with scriptural or scripturally based words, for birthday, Valentine's Day, Easter basket, Christmas, and "I love you" gifts. They became a strengthening force in the young man's spiritual life and increased his hunger for and knowledge of God's Word. In fact, his mother credits the influence of Christian contemporary music (and particularly Christian rock) with helping him to stand alone as a Christian in the public school in spite of strong peer pressure to rebel. Today he is involved on the national level of his denomination's youth ministry organization, and he loves the Lord with all his heart.

Another mother, a fairly new Christian with three teenage daughters, realized that just as it had taken the Lord some time to wean her from the world's influences in her life, so she could not expect her girls to develop instant Christian faith. Knowing her own children, she felt that asking them to withdraw cold turkey from their secular music would only alienate them from the heavenly Kingdom into which she was trying to love them. So she purchased plenty of Christian contemporary music for her own use and made time to take her girls to occasional Christian rock concerts. It wasn't very long before their conversations and attitudes began to reflect some of the values of the Christian music artists they were hearing.

In our society, music is a powerful tool. In *My Utmost for His Highest*, Oswald Chambers says, "Never make a principle out of your experience; let God be as original with other people as He is with you." Don't be narrow-minded about the music dilemma; instead, take advantage of its possibilities for making God real to your children.

5. To Push or Not to Push

Our daughter Karin was picking out melodies on the piano by ear at the age of three. By the time she was four or five, she was able to play with both hands and was often asked to do the offertory in junior church on Sunday morning. It wasn't long before she began formal lessons, which continued into high school. But her interest in playing for church and/or at school diminished. She considered her music a gift to be used solely for her own enjoyment and made her feelings very clear when we tried to encourage her to perform.

Then, during high school, she chose to quit piano lessons. We were disappointed. What a waste of her talent! But wanting to respect her decision, we tried to hide our emotions. I remember telling her, "Karin, we don't blame you for wanting to quit piano right now. We know you're really busy and tired of all the practicing. There'll be lots time later on if you should want to pick up where you've left off."

Guess what? Shortly after she was married, she resumed lessons, this time on the pipe organ! She eventually became organist at her church.

Christian parents need to pay more than lip service to the

concept of respecting their kids' decisions. Yes, some choices will have to be vetoed. If we know our children, however, we will be able to consider their interests, abilities, and feelings, trust their judgment, and allow them to mature into the individuals God intends them to be in His own time. There is a fine line between encouraging and pushing. Ask God to help you determine where that line is in any given situation.

6. Playing Favorites

Playing favorites is a high-risk game for parents, grandparents, aunts, and uncles, which almost always results in trouble.

Brittany and her family had been at Grandma and Grandpa's for Christmas. Joking with Aunt Jane and Uncle Jerry (always the life of the party), standing around the piano singing Christmas carols with the cousins, and opening all those wonderful gifts had added up to another great celebration.

When it was time to head home, Brittany stacked her treasures and began to put her coat on in the darkened hallway outside the kitchen. Hearing someone talking nearby—was that Grandma's voice?—she looked up.

Grandma and Grandpa, their backs to Brittany, stood in the kitchen talking to her youngest cousin, Mindy.

"Of course you know you've always been our favorite," Brittany heard Grandma say.

Swallowing hard as the tears welled up in her eyes, Brittany hurriedly finished putting on her coat, took her gifts, and slipped quietly out to the car to wait for Mom and Dad. All the way home Grandma's words rang in her ears.

For a young girl who had placed her grandparents on a

pedestal, it was a terrible experience. Yes, she had occasionally overheard snatches of conversation between relatives that implied Mindy was the favored one, but to hear her grandparents' bias stated outright was devastating. Years later, her stomach still sinks when she thinks back to that particular Christmas.

Remember the biblical story of Isaac, Rebekah, and their twin sons, Jacob and Esau (Genesis 27 and 28)? Jacob was his mother's favorite, so when it was time for Esau (the older twin by a few minutes) to receive Isaac's blessing, Rebekah helped Jacob deceive his nearly blind father and steal the blessing intended for Esau.

When Jacob later married and had children of his own, the pattern of favoritism repeated itself. Genesis 37:3 tells us that "Israel [Jacob] loved Joseph more than all his children, because he was the son of his old age" (KJV). The gorgeous coat of many colors Jacob gave to Joseph was probably the last in a long line of actions that demonstrated Joseph's favored status to his brothers. Jealousy erupted and Joseph's siblings plotted to rid themselves of "Daddy's little boy" by selling him into slavery and telling their father he was dead.

Perhaps we have not been involved in obvious acts of deceit as was Rebekah on behalf of Jacob; maybe we have not been as bold in our preferences for one child over another as Jacob was with Joseph. But favoritism can creep into our homes in a more subtle way: the comparison trap.

When we compare our kids with anyone—favorably or unfavorably—we are playing the favorites game. All too often we hear parents say:

"Why can't you keep your room picked up like your sister does?"

Or, "I don't know why you can't sit nicely at the table like your cousin Gretchen."

Or, "Can't you play as quietly [or run as fast, or sing as loud] as Jimmy?"

Such statements strike at the heart of a child's self-esteem and heighten sibling rivalry. No one wins, and the players (both children and parents) walk away discouraged and diminished by the exchange of negative sentiments.

We parents can learn from the mistakes of biblical characters such as the ones we have mentioned. In fact, 1 Corinthians 10:11 says, "All these things happened to them as examples—as object lessons to us—to warn us against doing the same things; they were written down so that we could read about them and learn from them. . . ."

I thank God when I think of the family in which I grew up. I knew I was loved, and I always felt that Jack, Kevin, and I had an equal share of our parents' affections. Sure, I remember Mom getting after Jack and me for ganging up on little "Cub" when he was making a general nuisance of himself. After all, we were older and should have known better. But I never felt my parents preferred one of us over the others.

A wise mother of seven children is known to have told them, "Always remember that my love for all of you has never been divided by seven; it has been multiplied by seven." It is important to *tell* children how special they are to us and that we appreciate their unique personalities.

This is how God relates to us, and we want to make real to our children the God who does not play favorites.

7. "I Don't Believe It, Not Mr. Churchman!"—Dealing With Sexual Abuse

Sometimes we tire of all the media coverage and school and television programming targeting the evils of sexual abuse. Perhaps it has been overdone, and, yes, there have been persons tragically, falsely accused of such behavior.

Nevertheless, the danger is real, and we need to talk with our children about it. They need to know how to say *no* and to run and tell someone if they have experienced an uncomfortable situation.

The thought of what happened more than thirty years ago still pops out of nowhere to haunt Barbara. She had been playing at her friend Mary's house on one of those hot, humid summer days. After Barbara, Mary, and Mary's older sister, Jenny, turned somersaults and cartwheels on the grass for a while, Mary and Jenny disappeared into the house to get a drink of water.

While they were gone, Barbara wandered into the garage, where Mary's dad was trying to fix the lawn mower. She watched him work for a few minutes, but before she realized what was happening, his hand was up her shorts and in her underpants.

"Little girls feel so good," Barbara remembers him saying. She froze, not daring to move. Fortunately Mary and Jenny came back out in a few minutes, so it wasn't a long, drawn-out encounter.

But Barbara's face must have shown her distress.

"Did Dad try something with you?" Jenny asked.

"Yes," Barbara answered in a whisper.

"Oh, he's always doing that." Jenny brushed the incident

aside. Her father—a husband, churchman, and professing Christian—was apparently abusing his daughters sexually on a regular basis.

Barbara never did tell her parents. Only after hearing many ugly stories of child abuse brought out into the open in the last few years was she able to confide to her brother the secret she had held locked inside for three decades.

It is easy to feel safe within our familiar circles of church, friends, and family, and thank goodness we are probably correct in doing so 99 percent of the time. But even people we trust do let us down or surprise us with deviant behaviors. Our children need us to open the door to conversations about their rights to the privacy of their bodies, and they need to know that if those rights are violated they can tell us without shame. Once again our explanations of this delicate subject must be tailored to their age levels and maturity and will deepen in content as they are repeated over the years.

8. Substance Abuse?—Not My Child!

A few years ago I noticed a billboard in a large airport corridor. It showed a mother and father sitting on an over-stuffed sofa. Blindfolds covered their eyes. Underneath the picture was the caption, "This is how some parents handle their kids' drug problems—BLINDFOLDED!"

No parents want to believe that *their* kids are involved in substance abuse or any other activity that threatens their well-being. But burying our heads in the sand only increases the danger to our youngsters.

Our Christian faith does not ensure that our children will never fall prey to the peer pressure that so often precedes the use of drugs, tobacco, and alcohol. If we know our children (*see* chapter 1) and pay attention to the three relational priorities (*see* chapter 2), we can help equip our kids to deal with that pressure. But if and when they do succumb, Christian parents have all the resources of God's wisdom, protection, and guidance at our disposal. And we must use them.

Sometimes prayer and a heart-to-heart talk will enable a child to work through the reasons for his or her experimentation with substance abuse. If the problem is deeper, counseling or counseling combined with a treatment program may be necessary. Many such resources are available in both the Christian and secular realms.

No matter what the situation, do not ignore symptoms that make you suspect your child needs help. And do not give up. Properly exercised, your Christian faith gives real hope for your child's recovery.

9. Snatched From Under Our Noses—The Problem of Cults

Carol Ann will never forget the intermission at a band concert when she visited with some Christian acquaintances whose daughter, Susan, had attended Carol Ann's junior high Sunday school class a few years previously. Susan's love of God and her commitment to Jesus Christ shone through in her sensitivity to the spiritual well-being of her peers. At one point Susan had spent considerable time consulting with Carol Ann about a friend's problems, in the process deepening her trust in Carol Ann as a teacher and confidante.

It had been years since the two had had any contact, what with college, summer jobs, and family activities intervening, so Carol Ann was horrified to hear that Susan had recently been baptized into a religious cult. She would not listen to advice from her parents or the pastor, and their home had become a battlefield.

Carol Ann clearly recalled a time twenty years ago when she had met some missionaries who represented the cult to which Susan now belonged. She had spent hours searching the Scriptures one weekend, checking out claims they based on Bible verses taken out of context and strengthening her personal relationship with Christ as a result. Now she wondered—perhaps God had been preparing her to help Susan. Close friends warned Carol Ann that interfering might make things worse. But Susan's eternal future was at stake, and Carol Ann felt led by the Holy Spirit to act. But how?

Prayer brought an idea to mind. A card would be a good way to come back into Susan's life. Carol Ann's carefully chosen "I'm so glad we're friends" greeting went in the mail the next day.

Continuing to ask God to guide her, Carol Ann found out where Susan was working and asked the Lord to help her set up a meeting. He did arrange the circumstances, and Susan showed an interest in sharing more than casually, so they made plans to talk after she finished work one evening.

Carol Ann and Susan talked and prayed together that night until 1:30 A.M.—and the next night, too. God was there with them, and Susan began to realize that Jesus is the only way to God and the Scriptures are His true revelation to human beings. She had a long, hard road ahead in extricating herself from the cult, but her parents eventually rejoiced in her return to the Christian faith.

Carol Ann still thanks God for the privilege of helping Susan. He sends us to one another in our times of need, for once we are His, no one can take us from Him. Remember:

1. God prepares us through our experiences to help others. He may use us when we least expect it, often with no advance notice. We need to be attuned to the Holy Spirit's leading.
2. When we build relationships with other people's kids (and encourage other adults to build relationships with our children), we weave safety nets that God uses to keep His own from falling.
3. A genuine faith shared by caring friends can help kids to focus on the Lord Jesus Christ even when they are tempted and struggling.
4. When God uses us to encourage others in their faith, we grow, too!

If your child is currently ensnared in a cult, don't give up. I have seen many adult children, whose parents have anguished over them in prayer, return to Christ. Sometimes it happens before their parents go home to heaven, sometimes after. In my childlike faith, I believe God lets those parents know their children are safe, once again, in His arms.

10. And Then There's TV. . . .

At the end of the day I like to put up my feet, prop a pillow under my head, wrap myself in a cozy comforter, and enjoy a good television program just as much as the next person. And there is nothing wrong with that—as long as God is in control of my viewing habits.

The apostle Paul tells us in the Book of Philippians to fix our thoughts "on what is true and good and right," to "think about things that are pure and lovely" (4:8). What a measuring stick for Christian adults to apply to our use of the television set! And what a tremendous guideline for Christian parents as we help our children choose appropriate programming and develop disciplined minds.

I am concerned for our children. We are bombarded by statistics from both Christian and non-Christian educators and psychologists that indicate our kids are spending too much of their lives in front of the tube. We are warned that we are spawning a generation of nonreading, nonthinking, physically inactive children who are greatly influenced by what they see. Some parents are paying attention; some are not.

Those statistics aside, it does not take much watching to discover that most of the sitcoms, soap operas (daytime and nighttime!), and MTV programs are supersaturated with violence and extramarital sex. If *we* are addicted to this kind of programming, our kids will be, too. What happens when they start to compare the values they see on our favorite TV programs with the principles we *say* we believe?

I know some psychologists deny it, but those programs must have an effect on kids' behavior. Josh McDowell, who has devoted much of his Christian life and ministry to working with youth, wrote in his 1987 book *Why Wait?* (Here's Life Publishers) that by the age of twenty, 81 percent of unmarried males and 67 percent of unmarried females have had sexual intercourse. And 87 percent of the teens who said they were sexually active had experienced sex before the age of seventeen.

Writing about the influence of the media on our children's sexual behavior, McDowell says:

The sexual "freedom" portrayed in today's entertainment is a joke made at the expense of human dignity. Sex without marriage so often leads to self-doubts, diseases, unwanted pregnancies, shattered emotions, manipulation, and exploitation. Such results are rarely portrayed on TV or in the movies because people don't want to hear about those things. . . . And since our culture demands entertainment that reflects its hopes—not its realities—our TV and movie screens will continue to bring us lies about sex. Teenagers whose minds are filled with these falsehoods will be increasingly influenced by them. . . . Parents must always be a resource of God's standards when a teenager needs an answer, but teenagers ultimately make their own decisions. The more they are taught from their early years to make proper choices, the easier it will be for them to stay on the right course when temptation comes.

It is so easy to think that young children are ignoring the TV set that is turned on for hours on end in so many homes. But they are listening, parents. . . .

Two-year-old Troy seemed to be content playing with his toys and looking at books in the family room as Mom relaxed with her favorite soap opera and a cup of coffee. It was standard afternoon procedure for mother and son.

As is the case on so many soaps, the characters changed partners as quickly as some people change sheets. This particular day found the heroine in bed with yet another man.

"Where's Jim?" Troy asked casually, looking up from his toys.

We think young children aren't paying attention, but they are! What do we want them to absorb in their early years?

Some Guidelines.

Some parents have agreed not to buy a television set for their homes. They occasionally allow their youngsters to indulge in TV viewing at Grandma's or when visiting a friend's house. Such parents, if they stick to their guns, may raise very creative children.

In his book *When TV Is a Member of the Family* (Abbey Press, 1981), however, Presbyterian pastor Edward N. McNulty comments:

> . . . passionate dumping of the set is [not] a very realistic response to television. Television is such a fact of modern life that to reject it completely is to live in a cultural ghetto, to become virtually an exile in your own country. . . . But to use it with no thought as to its consequences is to submit ourselves and our children to powers that will use us for their own ends—namely to make a profit from us regardless of what happens to us.

How do we use television thoughtfully? Here are some guidelines:

1. Be informed, ahead of time, about what programming is scheduled for a particular period of time. Having a game plan helps families to avoid the trap of turning on the TV automatically and remaining mindlessly glued to it, regardless of the content.

If we parents have checked out the viewing possibilities, we can suggest a scenario: "Let's finish the supper dishes, watch 'The Cosby Show,' then turn off the TV so we can play a game of Chutes and Ladders."

As we said before, many parents defend their children's

viewing habits, saying, "We know the set is on, but the kids aren't really watching. They're playing with something else."

So why not turn off the TV for a while? Periods of quiet in our homes provide wonderful opportunities for conversation, spontaneous family sing-alongs, or the pursuit of reading or hobbies. Who needs the constant din of unwatched programming as a backdrop for daily living—not to mention the electric bills it engenders? It is so easy to join the ranks of those who switch on the tube the minute they wake up in the morning and fall asleep with it still cranking out noise at night. Take the time to think about family viewing choices and how they affect the teaching of Christian values in your home.

2. Take advantage of educational programming. Public television has its drawbacks, but it provides numerous alternatives to commercial network fare.

3. Sit down with your children occasionally and watch programs you have selected together. Ask questions about what you are seeing so some interaction takes place. Your presence makes it possible to turn negative portions of the show into positives by interjecting Christian values and ideas or by discussing with your son or daughter a better way to handle the situation presented.

Ten-year-old Jamie loved to watch the "Dukes of Hazzard." You may recall the recklessness with which automobiles were driven on that show. Rather than tell Jamie the program was off limits, his parents opted to remind their impressionable son every so often that if Mom or Dad drove dangerously, they would end up in the hospital—or worse. They avoided mini-sermons, however; just a simple, "I'm so glad your daddy doesn't drive that way," was enough to get the point across.

4. Purchase a VCR and tape favorite shows for young children. When they want to watch TV, just put in a tape. Most little ones don't seem to know the difference.

The Christian video market is expanding rapidly. Many churches are developing their own video lending libraries. Some parents purchase tapes as gifts for their kids or to swap with other families. Used in moderation (and combined with family Bible reading, Bible storybooks, audio story cassettes, music, and, best of all, conversations with Mom and Dad), Christian videotapes can provide another great way to ground children in the Christian values we hold dear.

5. Some parents allow their youngsters to choose two thirty-minute programs a day. If they choose to do so, they can save up their time slots to watch a longer program instead.

6. Think twice before purchasing television sets for children's bedrooms. Individually owned sets (a) fragment the family physically—watching programs together is much better for everyone, (b) are a distraction in the bedroom, often the only quiet spot for homework, and (c) discourage children's participation in family group interaction.

Long-term exposure to non-Christian values from early childhood on has to influence the way children, even those from Christian homes, respond to life's decisions. It would be unfair to lay all the blame for the rampant lack of self-control so prevalent in our society at the feet of the television industry. Music, movies, books, peer pressure, magazines, and emotional upheaval caused by family stresses certainly contribute to the sad state of our world.

But how many times is the Christian family lifestyle the focus of positive television programming? How often have you seen Christians portrayed as strange or fanatical? I cringe when I realize how many people label all of Christendom by what they see presented on the tube. It hurts to see God and His people ridiculed. Imagine how this affects our children!

Be there for your children when the TV is on.

Whole books have been written on most of the ten tough problems we have mentioned in this chapter. For further ideas, check your church library or local Christian bookstore.

Just remember: Some, if not all, of these issues are sure to surface as you raise your family. God promised, in our instruction Manual, that we could ask freely for His wisdom (James 1:5). He is the God who never wastes anything but redeems even the worst of circumstances for our good if we are walking with Him (Genesis 50:20; Romans 8:28). We can trust Him, then, to help us use these tough problems as opportunities for making Him real to our children.

Questions for Thought

1. Am I aware of specific problems in my children's lives right now?

2. Do I know my children's friends and their families well

enough to communicate with them about important issues? If not, how can I get to know them better?

3. How does my use of broadcast and print media (television, newspapers, videotapes, books, magazines) affect my children's view of God? What changes can I make?

7

Into My Heart

Into my heart,
into my heart,
come into my heart, Lord Jesus.

That little chorus sung in Sunday schools all over the world introduces children to the idea of inviting Jesus to live within them. They may not fully understand this abstract concept at first, but once the seed is planted, it grows and can be nurtured into beautiful lives given to God.

We think our six-year-old niece, JoAnn, a very wise and wonderful member of our family, understood what it meant to have Jesus in her heart. She will always be six years old to us, even though her friends graduated from high school this year, because JoAnn is not with us anymore. She is at home with Jesus.

Several months after JoAnn was born, doctors discovered her heart was defective. She breezed through her first open-heart surgery at the tender age of four. Two years later the surgery was repeated. But this time complications set in, and following three weeks of ups and downs within the walls of the intensive care unit, the roller coaster ride ended, and we lost JoAnn. She had the best medical care possible, but it wasn't enough.

As a family we remember her sense of humor, the twinkle in her eye, her determination, her insight, and her childlike faith.

One day when JoAnn was four, she announced to her daddy that she had invited Jesus into her heart. How we laughed and cried later that year when after her first surgery she exclaimed, "Mommy, when the doctor opened me up, did he find Jesus or batteries?" (Remember those dolls with battery compartments in their chests? Kids are thinking every minute!)

One day while visiting Grandma, JoAnn sat on the living room floor twisting and turning the pieces of a puzzle, apparently engrossed in what she was doing as Mom and Grandma talked. Their church was hosting some special meetings, and the conversation centered on the sermon topic of the previous evening. Looking up from her puzzle, JoAnn offered, "He *did* say that Jesus died for our sins." She knew precisely what Jesus had done for her!

Questions and thoughts about heaven surfaced often.

"Mommy, when I go to heaven, I'm going to tie a rope around our house and take it with me."

"Mommy, will Baby Moses be all grown up when I get to heaven?"

"Mommy, does it rain in heaven? Will Jesus give us umbrellas?"

JoAnn's grandpa had died, and she knew he was in heaven, but like most young children she did not quite understand the finality of death. Several months after his homegoing, she asked her mother, "Isn't it about time for Grandpa to come back?"

There is nothing quite like the thrill of seeing little children put two and two together. JoAnn, like others her age, didn't always come up with four, but she was close. One day when she was on her way to visit Grandma, she slipped a handmade valentine for Grandpa in her pocket. She gave it to Grandma with explicit instructions to deliver it to Grandpa when she went to heaven. After all, if Grandpa was in heaven, wouldn't it be logical from a child's perspective for Grandma to go there next?

There was no doubt in our minds that God was real to JoAnn. One day while she ate lunch she commented, "I'll bet Grandpa has met Mary and Joseph by now."

JoAnn has met them, too. That's our faith.

Great Beginnings

Like JoAnn, Karl was born to parents whose primary goal is to make God real to their children. As an infant he was rocked to sleep in his mother's arms as she sang songs about Jesus.

At nineteen months of age, Karl loves "Jes-a." When it is story time, he makes a beeline for the book basket and by-passes all the other volumes to get to the one that tells him Jesus loves him. He likes that idea.

We need to begin early to introduce our children to Jesus. Doing so will pay big dividends later on.

In a cover story appearing in the April 13–15, 1990, edition of *USA Today*, Nanci Hellmich zeroes in on the importance of building a foundation for a child's developing faith. She offers these tips from the experts she surveyed:

- Start instruction in your faith early.
- Start at home.
- Don't pretend to know all the answers.

Adds Hellmich, "The key to working with preschoolers and young children is to inform without overwhelming them."

JoAnn, Karl, and many others like them show us children

can develop relationships with Jesus at their own levels of understanding very early in life. They love knowing that God created them as unique human beings. They love stories of the Baby Jesus who grew up to heal the sick, make the deaf to hear and the blind to see. They love being helpers. And they love knowing that Jesus loves them.

To designate seven years of age the traditional age of accountability seems to be a man-made idea. According to Anita Schorsch's book *Images of Childhood* (Main Street Press, 1985), the number seven separated

> the infant child from the reasonable child and the toy-playing child from the reading child and servant, ending the period of "effeminacy" and beginning the rite of passage for boys—a time when apprenticeship contracts were first to be drawn up. It was a time, in later centuries, of clothing change (generally from dresses to breeches), and coincided with the religious crisis which parents stirred in the child of seven.

Whenever a child shows interest in belonging to the Lord, the time is right, whether he or she is four or fourteen. But the decision must be his or her own. Be sure your child does not feel pushed into accepting Christ to please you.

If a child says he has asked Jesus into his heart, it is a good idea to ask about the experience. The answers will tell you where the child is in terms of his understanding, and you can proceed gently to clear up any questions or confusion that might exist in his mind.*

---

* For help in explaining the plan of salvation to children, *see Keeping Your Kids Christian*, edited by Marshall Shelley (Vine Books, 1990). *See* especially chapter 11, "How to Lead a Child to Christ," by Luis and Pat Palau.

A Word About Special Needs Children

The Sunday school lesson for the week told of Jesus healing the lame man.

"Do any of you know someone who is lame?" asked the teacher. Her second-graders shook their heads. They knew no one who was lame.

She rephrased the question.

"Do any of you know someone who can't walk?"

No, they didn't know anyone who couldn't walk.

She tried again.

"Do you know someone who can't run like you do, someone who has to sit in a wheelchair?"

Finally it dawned on the children: Their classmate, Nathaniel, couldn't do those things. He was multiply handicapped. Born with cerebral palsy, he couldn't walk, talk, or learn as his peers could. But he was just one of the gang! They did not think of him as lame or handicapped.

It was obvious to the teacher that Nathaniel's presence in her Sunday school class was a blessing to the other children, to herself, and to Nathaniel. She does not know how much he is capable of understanding; neither do the experts. Only God knows. But the children's accepting and helpful attitude toward their friend could certainly be a channel of God's love.

Many Nathaniels in the world need to hear how much Jesus cares about them. Acceptance by their peers, regardless of their special needs, can occur naturally if adults have the foresight to realize the potential good for everyone involved.

Is God real to the special needs child? He can be. Perhaps his or her level of understanding will never go beyond that of a child, but as we have seen, children can know God loves them through songs, through His Word, and through the gentle touches of the Body of Christ in action.

Christian adults need to model the love of God to persons with special needs, adults and children alike. We need to make the Nathaniels of our world welcome in our churches. Our love and concern can help their weary parents, but we usually end up on the receiving end of an even greater blessing. Best of all, our examples of Christian love can help make God real to *all* the youngsters who are watching.

Leaving It Up to Them—A Myth

Some parents do not believe in training a child from infancy in the way he or she should go spiritually. There may be several lines of reasoning behind their persuasion.

Sometimes, in an attempt to keep peace with both sets of in-laws or between themselves, parents who come from divergent backgrounds send their children to Daddy's church one week and Mommy's the next. These parents usually reason that the children will be able to appreciate both denominations (or faiths, if they are not the same) and will choose for themselves in adolescence or adulthood. This reminds me of a little boy who explained to his friends at holiday time that he was "Jewish and a little bit Christmas"!

Other parents choose to skip the whole idea of Sunday school and church and strive to raise morally upright children without benefit of religious training. In many such cases, Mom and Dad have been turned off by a legalistic, "do's and don'ts" religious experience themselves or worry that a child will be frightened by religion.

"If they want to attend church later on in their lives, that's up to them," these parents frequently say.

Then there are parents who know better but want to use Sunday as a day to relax. Sunday school attendance is hit or miss at best, and if the kids do go, they are often dropped off at the door and picked up before morning worship. Involvement in the Body of Christ is seldom a family affair.

If I were a gambler, I would say the odds in the aforementioned vignettes are against producing children with strong religious faith. Certainly these views do not reflect the scriptural mandates for raising our children to love and serve God.

Kevin, a preschool student, was a bubbly four-year-old with personality plus. His mom and dad were totally turned off by even the slightest mention of going to church. They weren't going to get involved in that "crazy stuff."

Kevin had a praying grandfather who told him all about Jesus whenever he visited from out of town. But although Kevin wanted nothing more in the whole world than to go to Sunday school, his only opportunities came when his visiting Grandpa was able to take him.

As always, St. Patrick's Day was a big celebration at preschool that year. The children learned about St. Patrick, Blarney Castle, shamrocks, and the Blarney stone. Each child was allowed one wish as he or she leaned over to kiss the class version of the famous stone, and the teachers recorded what each child said to share with Mom and Dad.

Can you guess what Kevin wished for? Yes, he wanted to go to Sunday school!

In His marvelous grace and certainly because of the prayers of a faithful grandfather, God moved in a very special way in Kevin's life. As a teenager, he has given his heart to Jesus, has many Christian friends, and is actively involved in his church. Someday he hopes to see his parents walk closely with God, too.

We do not let our children *choose* whether or not they want to eat nutritious meals; good parents consider it part of their job to see that their children have a balanced diet. And I haven't heard of too many parents who offer their youngsters options about looking both ways before they cross the street; safety considerations make that rule a must.

How much more we need to be concerned about instilling in our children the guidelines and protection for their future that early religious training provides! Without it, they are on dangerous ground physically, emotionally, mentally, socially, and spiritually.

Encouraging Children in the Faith

As I mentioned before, it is never appropriate to shove a child into accepting Jesus into his or her heart. That decision must be made according to God-given free will.

But in addition to knowing our children, establishing our three top priorities, offering loving discipline, developing good lines of communication, and making family life FUN, we can take several specific steps to enhance our youngsters' early religious training and increase their understanding of God's reality and personal interest in their lives.

Accent the Positive.

I am sure we have all listened to folks who moan and groan about Christmas and birthday gift giving and would like to abolish it altogether.

"There's not a thing that woman needs."

"He's got everything."

"It's hard enough to buy for our own family, but having to get gifts for the relatives is more than we can handle."

Having to do something is one thing; *wanting* to do it is another. When people give because they *have* to, what's the point?

The same is true in our relationship with God. Do we *have* to go to church on Sunday, or do we *want* to worship our Lord? Do we *have* to say our prayers, or do we enjoy spending time in His presence? Do I hurry to get my Bible reading over with, or am I filled with hunger and thirst for more spiritual food and drink? Are our church commitments fulfilled out of obligation, or are they the natural outgrowth of our love for Christ and our desire to please Him in appreciation for His gifts to us?

Our children are watching. Do they see positive, love-motivated Christianity or negative, dutiful religion?

In addition to checking how positively we represent our own attitudes toward our faith, we may need to give up using God-related fear tactics as disciplinary tools. Avoid statements such as, "Jesus doesn't like it when you hit your brother," and, "You'd better be good; God is watching everything you do." Those phrases and others like them present God as a drill sergeant ready to jump all over the recruit who is the least little bit out of line. Don't forget, God has placed parents in authority over children, and it is *our* job to deal with disciplinary issues, drawing on the wisdom of His Holy Spirit.

When a child does something wrong it is sufficient to say, "I am very upset with what I see," and to administer further discipline if the situation calls for it. Bringing God into the picture as a sledgehammer—or even as a gentle poke—at this point will only alienate a child from Him. Later on, when things are going smoothly, we can read stories and make positive comments to encourage acceptable behavior that pleases God.

Children's views of God are frequently carried over into adulthood, affecting how they relate to Him and to their parents and children, as well as to the institutional Church and Christian friends and acquaintances, long after their viewpoints on other issues have matured. A distorted conception of God is difficult to bring back into focus and is often the cause of much unnecessary mental, emotional, and relational suffering.

Fear Strikes Back: Emphasize God's Love.

Do you recall hearing sermons that scared you half to death? I do—they were all the hellfire-and-brimstone variety. The style in which they were delivered was enough to frighten even the most godly person. Yet it seemed at the time as if all that shouting and pulpit banging paid off; many who listened cried and committed themselves to Jesus Christ. I was one of them.

Did I say the right words? How could I know I was saved? I am a firstborn child, the natural worrier in the family, the one who wants to do everything just right. So despite my Christian mother's reassurances, my fear-filled experience reflected my personality makeup.

After I accepted Jesus into my heart, I continued to hear more fiery sermons. *Does the minister mean* me? *Do I need to raise my hand and go forward—again? Must I repent of my sins—again? Do I need to rededicate my life to Christ—again?*

Today I love Jesus with all my heart, but it is still difficult for me to overcome the often false guilt of the "I have to's" and live in the joy of the "I want to's."

We will be talking more about faith-related fears in a few moments. For now, though, remember that fears about God instilled in our childhood can strike back in later years. As we

begin to teach our little ones about God, we need to concentrate on His unending love for them evidenced by:

1. His desire for a relationship with each of us
2. His provision for the forgiveness of our sins through
   Jesus, which is ours for the asking

As children mature in their knowledge and experience of
God's love, they will understand what they need to know
about the consequences of sin and disobedience. If they have
learned to love Jesus first, the desire for fellowship with Him
can draw them back to the fold even when they have strayed.

Establish a Family Home Altar.

In Christian circles we often hear references to the importance of establishing a family home altar—a deliberate time
for the family to share in Bible reading and prayer. (Your
denominational tradition may call it something else—family
devotions, family worship, etc.)

By *deliberate* I do not mean *rigid*. Family busy-ness ebbs and
flows, and flexibility is as important in this area of making God
real to our children as it is in many others. Two keys to
success in this endeavor are (1) sensitivity to the Holy Spirit's
leading for your particular family, and (2) a measure of parental self-discipline. If the family gets away from spending devotional times together for a brief period, be faithful to ease
back into the pattern as soon as possible, without presenting
it as an "ought" or a negative.

Some parents use bedtime as a family devotional period.
Others may set aside fifteen or twenty minutes when family
members can engage in in-depth Bible study and prayer.

Many families find it fairly easy to offer sentence prayers around the dinner table, perhaps holding hands while they take turns talking to God.

Whatever works for your family, God will honor. Just remember, establishing a family home altar is easier when your children are young. If the pattern is firmly established by the time they hit the more independent years of adolescence, they will probably continue to cooperate willingly or at least offer less resistance.

If your kids are older, begin where they are. After-school conversations may lead into natural opportunities to pull out the Bible and say, "Let's look it up," or, "Let's pray for your friend right now."

Please note three words of caution. First, encourage family members to participate in the family home altar, but never impose it on anyone. Here again, children may go through different stages of willingness to take part, and methods of family worship may need to be varied accordingly. If when your children are older they prefer to pray privately, a simple prayer at the dinner table can help to bring concerns before God as a family in a casual, nonthreatening way. Simpler still (and an excellent starter for the family just beginning to establish a home altar), add a PS to the regular table grace, briefly mentioning a specific need or adding a personal petition or two for an individual.

What if mom or dad is uncomfortable with the concept of a family altar?

Terry is a very private person. He has been a Christian for many years and always leaves an hour early for the office in order to share a quiet time with the Lord. But whenever his wife, Lynn, suggested that they pray together or read the Bible and pray with the children, he withdrew. So Lynn established a family altar with the kids, making sure they knew Daddy loved Jesus and had his own quiet time, as well. Insisting on Terry's presence or placing guilt on him for not participating would only have produced tension and unhappiness. Lynn can hope and pray that continued openness to God on Terry's part will give him the desire, someday soon, to share in his family's spiritual togetherness.

If one parent is not a Christian, the other should establish a family altar with the children if possible. The Christian parent, however, needs to avoid flaunting these devotional times, assuming a "holier than thou" attitude, or fostering disrespect for the non-Christian parent because he or she will not participate. Peter's advice is helpful here: "Be beautiful . . . in your hearts, with the lasting charm of a gentle and quiet spirit which is so precious to God" (1 Peter 3:4). And in 1 Corinthians 7:12–17, Paul suggests that the loving attitude of a Christian mate may draw his or her non-Christian spouse to the Lord. Quiet, purposeful application of the principles we have discussed for instituting a family home altar should give no cause for a non-Christian mate to feel pushed away or rejected by the rest of the family.

The second caution? Do not try to have family altar when everyone is rushed. Timing is important! I can remember Mom gathering the three of us together when we were ready to run out the door to school in the morning. I don't think I was always in the mood to concentrate on the words of the chorus we sang, and I know my brother almost died of embarrassment as his friend stood outside waiting for him.

Third, never—no, never—allow dinner to get cold because you have insisted on a lengthy devotional reading or prayer. The entire family will be mad at you, and they will be more impatient with family devotions the next time. If you sense that the home altar needs to be longer on a given day, plan to have it when the family schedule allows, rather than trying to cram it in and alienate your family.

Let Your Children Hear You Pray.

It is really crucial for children to hear us pray. They need to know that prayer is a real part of our everyday lives and that we depend on God for everything.

When we pray, then, we should:

- Speak simply and honestly; kids know when we are sincere—and when we aren't.
- Forget the "thees" and "thous"; we can talk naturally to God.
- Be brief.
- Zero in on the specifics. Instead of saying, "God, please forgive all my sins," we can ask Him to forgive us for losing our tempers when the rice boiled over or for speaking unkindly to the newspaper boy. It is fine for our children to see us as less than perfect. If God still loves us even though we often fall far short of His plan, they know there is hope for them, too.

A word of caution: Save the really deep concerns for your personal quiet time with God. Exposure to serious family or financial problems before they are mature enough to handle them can make children unnecessarily and agonizingly anxious.

Offer Faith-Building, Hands-On Experiences.

Little ones are eager to learn, forever curious, always on the move, and into everything. Experts in the field of early childhood education tell us that an individual's greatest period of physical and intellectual growth takes place during the preschool years.

The wise parent, then, offers a child as many faith-building, hands-on experiences as possible in the process of trying to make God real. Don't just *tell* children the story of the little boy who shared his five loaves and two fish with Jesus. Pretend to climb the "mountain" (stairs?) with them to see Jesus. Sit down on the "grass" (rug?), and taste and feel the little boy's lunch of tuna and bread you have packed for your own noon meal. If you really have the time to get into it, dress up in robes and sandals. The kids will love it, and they will remember that story forever.

Acting out a Bible story for Grandma and Grandpa, taking cookies to a neighbor to demonstrate "Love one another" (1 John 4:7 NIV), and playing together with Noah's ark in the tub are all visual, tactile ways to make God's Word come alive. I know it is not possible to do this all the time, but years from now the memories of even a few such events will be magnified a hundred times in your child's treasury of happiness and positive feelings about God.

Take Advantage of Bedtime for Making God Real.

As each day drew to a close at the Chall household, the children took baths, brushed teeth, and rested sleepy (and sometimes not so sleepy) little heads on soft pillows as Mom or Dad tucked each small person into bed for the night. This was our quiet time for Bible stories and prayer, for sharing thoughts and feelings, and for telling about some of the day's activities that may have been overlooked around the dinner table.

It was obvious one night when Kristine was just learning to pray that she had caught on to her big sister's game—keeping Mom in the bedroom for as long as possible. After saying her bedtime prayer-poem, she went on to ask Jesus to bless each of her friends and family members.

Then she really got into thanking God: "Dear Jesus, thank You for my bed, my dresser, my toys, the light, my clothes. . . ." She continued until she had just about exhausted every item in the room. Then, with one eye peeking at me from behind the little hands she had kept folded in front of her face, she began on the kitchen. "Thank You for the stove, the sink, the refrigerator—and maybe for the toaster?" Her sister's giggles clued me in. We all look back on those wonderful days with warmth.

I know just how exhausted parents get as night falls. It can be a real temptation to rush through those bedtime rituals, but resist it. (As a mother who has been there, I would like to add at this point, "Blessed is the tired husband who shares this responsibility with his tired wife!")

My phone rang last night. Our grown daughter Karin, now a mother of two, was on the other end.

"Oh, Mom," she sighed. "I just have to tell you this."

It had been one of those busy days. Now the toys were picked up, and the children were bathed and tucked in bed. Katie had said her prayers, and it was three-year-old Ben's turn.

Karin, a bit weary, lay down on the bed beside him. After they prayed and Mommy had added some extra "God blesses" to satisfy Ben, he looked into her eyes.

"I touch your hair?"

Karin nodded.

"Hair," came the gentle affirmation as his little fingers patted softly.

The little game continued.

"Eye."

"Ear."

"Nose." Ben giggled.

"Cheek." He placed his small hand tenderly on her face.

Karin smiled, and as she did so, Ben ever so gently reached up with his other hand. Holding her face with both hands he said, "You're wonderful, Mom."

What a way to end the day!

Never Frighten a Child Unnecessarily.

Just a few weeks ago, I heard a preacher on Christian radio refer to a special message he had received from God by opening his Bible at random (and taking a verse out of context). I thought this emphasis had long passed away.

During my childhood, it was common to hear from the pulpit that God speaks to His people in this way. Often I would jump into bed, take my Bible, open it, and whatever verse my eyes fell upon became my verse for the day.

I can remember as if it were yesterday. My mom and dad were visiting friends for the evening, and I was at home babysitting for my two younger brothers. When I took my Bible and opened it to find my message from God, my eyes fell on the verse, "Verily I say unto thee, To day shalt thou be with me in paradise" (Luke 23:43 KJV).

I just knew I was going to die—today! I ran to the phone and called my mom.

"Please come home, I'm afraid," I pleaded.

"But, honey, you'll be fine," she comforted.

Explain as she would about taking things out of context, nothing satisfied me. If I was going to die, I wanted my mom and dad to be with me.

The tears were flowing down my cheeks as I continued to beg, "Oh, please come home."

Come home they did, and right away. The half hour it took them to get home seemed like an eternity. Once my mom and dad were with me, I could finally drift off to sleep. And when I saw the light of a new day, I understood.

Other issues in the spiritual realm can also be scary for small children.

It was circle time during Sunday school hour. Three-year-old Andrew was listening intently as his teacher told of Jesus' ascension into heaven.

"Don't you just love Jesus?" she asked the group of little ones sitting before her on the rug. "Someday we'll all go to heaven. We'll be able to see Jesus and talk to Him."

An anxious look came over Andrew's face.

"My mommy won't *let* me go," he said with certainty.

Why *wouldn't* the thought of heaven be a bit frightening to a child when the thought of eternity is intimidating even to many Christian adults? The fears of change, of the unknown, and of separation from loved ones that sometimes plague grown-ups are even more scary to children.

Please don't get me wrong. I know from the experience of others close to me that God sends His Holy Spirit to comfort and reassure His chosen ones when they face death. Jesus is with us all the way.

But children do not have an adult's storehouse of life wisdom to help them deal with the big issues of death, suffering and pain, heaven and hell. Even repetition of the old rote prayer "Now I lay me down to sleep," with its heart-thumping phrase, "If I should die before I wake," is enough to give some little ones nightmares.*

So how can we make God real to our children and yet avoid scaring them?

Much depends on the way parents and teachers present concepts to children. If the adults in a child's life believe heaven will be wonderful, the child will probably catch their enthusiasm. If adults face suffering or death with courage, cheerfulness, and trust that God will see them through, the youngsters around them can face it, too. This will be true especially if those same adults are sensitive enough to watch for questions in children's eyes, voices, and actions and answer them honestly, thus relieving many fears.

Children can be told, for example, that there are really only three ways to die: through an accident, an illness, or old age. Reassurances about Mom's and Dad's care over them in preventing accidents, about the availability of excellent medical care and modern medicines, and about the many years until they will be old can go a long way toward calming the fear of death. No, we can make no guarantees to our kids, but Jesus used a parable to tell us to occupy until He comes, to go on living prudently and in tune with Him, yes, but *normally* while we carry on His business (*see* Luke 19:13). (And that thought, incidentally, can help older children to handle their uncertainties and unease about prophecies and the Second Coming of Christ.)

"Mommy, what's heaven like?" Four-year-old Katie's question surprised her mother. Not sure what to say, Mom told Katie that heaven is a beautiful place God has prepared for people who love Jesus to go to when they die.

---

* Many books of prayers for children are available at your local Christian bookstore.

"It's a place where everyone is happy and Jesus takes care of us. The streets are made of gold, and there are lots of pretty jewels like the diamond in Mommy's ring and like pearls and rubies," she continued.

"Where do people who *don't* love Jesus go when they die?"

"The Bible tells us they go to a very sad place called hell," replied Mom, but she didn't dwell on the details.

Young children have no concept of time or space, so Katie thought she would be going to heaven right away. Mom reassured her that it would probably be a long, long time before she would go.

That night during prayer time, Katie paused for several seconds before she started to pray. "This is a hard one, Mom. I have to think about it first."

Finally she began:

> Dear Jesus,
> Thank You that we're almost in heaven. Please help Mommy to remember to bring the toys so me and Ben can play when we get there. We like the diamonds, but we don't like the "sad place" and I want to see Baby Jesus. We like the gold, and when my clothes get all dirty, please buy me some new clothes. Amen.

Katie's parents had a good chuckle that evening—but they had reason to be proud, too. Their efforts were making God real to their child!

Questions for Thought

1. Are the overall atmospheres in my church and home fear and duty-oriented, or do my children experience positive

acceptance and applications of biblical truths that attract them to God through Jesus Christ? If change needs to take place, what can I do to help?

2. Bearing in mind each family member's God-given individuality, how can I incorporate prayer, Bible reading, and Christian music naturally into the flow of our daily schedule?

3. Is bedtime in our home exhausting? Hurried? Happy? Warm? A shared and sharing experience? How can I take full advantage of bedtime to help make God real to my children?

8

—

Help Wanted

As I review the past seven chapters, I realize anew what a huge responsibility we have in the task of Christian parenting!

But what joys and privileges are ours, as well. One day not too long ago, I happened to overhear part of a conversation between my mom and my father-in-law, both of whom have been senior citizens for many years.

"You know, May," said Wes's dad, "sometimes I don't think these 'golden years' are all they're cracked up to be. I'm afraid we *had* our golden years a long time ago. Trouble is, we didn't realize it!"

Sometimes tired parents are unaware that they are smack-dab in the middle of what they will look back upon as their golden years—years when they were surrounded by their children and intensely involved in those children's lives.

Raising kids and making God real to them requires large investments of time.

"No kidding!" I can just hear someone saying. "My

husband works hard to earn enough money to keep a roof over our heads and our family fed and clothed. It takes a lot of time to run a household, not to mention all the other things I'm supposed to help with in church, at school, and in the community. Sometimes there aren't enough hours in the day to do justice to everything and everyone, including grandparents, aunts, uncles, cousins, special friends, the kids' friends and activities, and the neighbor down the street who just came home from the hospital. Where do I get all the hours and energy I need to make God real to my children?"

I will be the first to admit that it is easy to see what should be done but tougher to find the resources to accomplish it all. When the dishes are stacked high, your feet stick to the floor as you walk, Johnny needs help with his homework, and Grandpa is coming for supper, it is hard to make the time to read little Alice a Bible story or take Lindsay for a ride in her stroller.

As in all of the parenting issues we have discussed in this book, the word *balance* is pertinent here. Sometimes we have days, even weeks, when life's external circumstances deny us the time and ability to focus on the creative and fun activities of making God real to our children. Even during those periods, however, it is important to keep as close to the Lord as possible so we can listen for His cues in helping our families through rushed or turbulent situations. The lessons learned during these rough spots can stick just as well as the ones offered in the gentleness of cozy family times.

Another factor enters in here. Children definitely need our time and attention, but they also need time to develop resources within themselves. They require a healthy balance of busy-ness with significant others and quietness when they are free of organized activity—times to listen to the silence, do what they feel like doing, and just BE.

Quiet at-home times can help in preparing children to be silent and relaxed before God in prayer, study, and worship as adults. The Scriptures remind us, "Be still, and know that I am God" (Psalms 46:10 KJV).

Later, Honey, Later!

For today's parents, the danger of smothering kids with too much of our time and attention is much less than the danger of becoming so busy in the ordinary rush of adult pursuits that we brush aside our children's requests to play games, read stories, or examine their building projects. How often do we hear ourselves saying, "I'm almost finished with this, honey. I'll be right there"? But we may lose the moment, never getting around to responding to a child's request. Our intentions are good; we just forget or are interrupted.

When our children were younger, I learned this lesson the hard way. In western New York State we have a saying, "If you don't like the weather, wait a minute—it will change." One summer in particular, on several occasions I hurried to get my house in order during the morning hours so Karin, Kristine, Tom, and I could head up to the lake for a day at the beach. Each time, once I had finally packed lunch and loaded all the kids into the car, the skies clouded over, and we had to cancel our plans. So I learned to take advantage of sunny mornings. The housework could wait.

When They're Older, I'll Have Lots of Time

Don't count on it! I can remember feeling that once my children were all in school, I'd have plenty of time to accomplish my household jobs and do what I wanted to do. In reality, their school attendance and increased participation at church meant I was *more* involved in spreading myself among the activities of three youngsters of different ages, abilities, and interests.

But it is so important for parents to be available to listen to and share with each child. I will never forget the night a lovely woman came up to me after a seminar and told me, with tears flooding her eyes, of the little girl, Jeanie, she had lost suddenly to meningitis at the tender age of seven. At that point in her life, she had not understood the importance of giving her child the gift of herself. She was always on the go—choir practice, women's groups, this committee meeting or that one. Many weeks found her away from home almost every evening.

"Spend time with your children while you can," she urged me. "I wish so much that I had. I'm still haunted by Jeanie's pleas: 'Mommy, can't you stay home tonight?'"

Guard those precious moments. As children enter school, the time they spend away from home increases dramatically. Family altar, fun days and Sundays, vacations, and even dinner times when everyone is present around the table become harder and harder to schedule unless parents adjust their lifestyles to make room for what counts.

Time has a way of running out for each of us, some sooner, some later. God does not want His children to be fearful, but we need to decide what is important and act upon those decisions. We have only the present time to be with our youngsters and make God real to them. Let's not permit it to sift through our fingers.

Looking Ahead—It Scares Me Half to Death!

When our children are small, it can be intimidating to look down the road toward those teenage years. The news and stories we hear from older friends about drug and alcohol abuse, the dating scene, and general rebellion can make us wonder how our families will ever survive. Rest assured. If we do our homework:

1. We'll grow right along with our children.
2. God will be there for us and for our kids.
3. The teen years can be great years.
4. The worst thing we can do is worry!

Was That "No" I Heard?

Linda and Wendy grew up in a close-knit family. To the casual observer it seemed as though they were always surrounded by adult relatives, many of whom had never married. Consequently, even cousins were few and far between.

When it came time for church, the girls were never allowed to sit with their friends—not on Sunday mornings, Sunday evenings, or during Wednesday-night prayer meetings. Perhaps some of their later rebellion against giving God first place in their lives stemmed from being smothered by parents who had not learned that appropriate family togetherness requires balance and constant adjustment.

Kids need breathing space. They cannot be under our thumbs every minute. I think sitting together in church as families is wonderful, but there should be some occasions, maybe during less-formal church gatherings, when children can join their friends.

Parents need to understand that Christian parenting also involves allowing youngsters, depending on their ages and maturity levels, the freedom to make some choices.* The home is the perfect practice field. If parents make all the decisions relative to their children, what will their kids do when they are away from Mom and Dad's watchful eyes? We need to let go gradually so our children grow into independent, thinking, confident adults who exhibit self-control and an enthusiasm for playing the game of life in a way that pleases God.

A tennis coach invests lots of time and energy in his players. The coach has the right to say and do what he wants before the match, but once a game begins, he can say nothing—or risk being thrown off the court. The player is completely on his own.

Christian parenting is like that. We want our kids to be able to make it on their own when coaching time is over.

Parents who try to keep their children reined in too tightly are raising young people who will be ripe for the cults and peer group pressures.

* *See* " 'I Can't Make Up My Mind!'—Helping Kids Make Choices" in chapter 6.

Need Help? Look What Our Instruction Manual Has to Offer

How good God was to give us the Bible! Remember 2 Timothy 3:16, 17?

> The whole Bible was given to us by inspiration from God and is useful to teach us what is true and to make us realize what is wrong in our lives; it straightens us out and helps us do what is right. It is God's way of making us well prepared at every point, fully equipped to do good to everyone.

We can be fully equipped and well prepared as parents. Check the following guidelines. God didn't leave out anything!

1. We need to live each day in prayer communion with God. Jesus did (Mark 1:35).
2. Through bold, continual prayer we will receive the mercy and grace we need to deal with every situation (Hebrews 4:16).
3. Help comes from our great Creator God (Psalms 121:2).
4. We can trust God for everything. If we put Him first, He will lead us (Proverbs 3:5, 6).
5. God wants us to give Him all our cares and worries. He is concerned about us (1 Peter 5:7).
6. Children are God's gifts to us. We need to let Him be the focus of our families' lives. If we rely on Him, we can sleep well, knowing He cares (Psalms 127:1–3).

7. If we show love to family members (and others), their imperfections will not seem so great (1 Peter 4:8).

8. The Bible was given to teach us the truth so we can determine right from wrong (2 Timothy 3:15–17).

9. Christian parents must present a united front (Matthew 12:25).

10. We need to listen to our children before judging them (Proverbs 18:13).

11. We need to give our bodies to God, live lives that please Him, and love others as Christ loved us (Romans 12:1, 2; Ephesians 5:1, 2).

12. We must view the events recorded in the Bible as examples for our instruction. Many human beings have faced temptations similar to ours. But God is faithful; He will not allow us to be tempted beyond our abilities to resist through the power of His Holy Spirit (1 Corinthians 10:11, 13).

13. The husband-wife relationship is the key to healthy parent-child relationships (Ephesians 5:21–23).

14. Within a marriage there is no room for repaying evil for evil. We need to show compassion for each other, be courteous and of one mind, and live together in harmony so our prayers are not hindered (1 Peter 3:1–9).

15. Solomon recognized God's place in his life. He knew God alone was wise and asked for an understanding heart and the ability to know right from wrong. We can ask for God's wisdom in parenting our children (1 Kings 3:5–14, 28; James 1:5).

16. The Bible defines wisdom that comes from heaven as: pure, gentle, peace-loving, easy to deal with, full

of mercy and good deeds, without quarreling or discord, and sincere (James 3:13–18).

Other Help Is Available, Too

In addition to our instruction manual, the ever-present power of the Holy Spirit, prayer, the advice and prayers of trusted Christian friends, pastors, and counselors, church programs, and the tapes, books, and videos currently available in Christian bookstores, other helps are available for Christian parents.

Christian Elementary and Secondary Education.

The Christian school movement in our community came into its own after our children were well established in their respective public schools. But I have had opportunities to visit several Christian schools and talk to parents, teachers, and administrators. I have observed atmospheres of mutual love and respect between children, parents, and staff members. How wonderful when the adults a child interacts with can emulate the love of God and are encouraged to talk about the Lord in the normal course of conversation and subject-related discussions in the classroom!

Christian schools usually provide smaller classes, permitting teachers to offer more individualized attention to their students. And most of the schools I have visited seem to hold a "back to the basics" philosophy of education where God is central and discipline is administered to elicit cooperation and respect.

The nation's newspapers headline story after story of poor test scores, escalating disciplinary problems, crime, and teacher burnout within our public schools. Kids, our country's most valuable resource, are slipping through the cracks.

"But," I can hear some parents saying, "children need to be exposed to the real world. We can't protect them all of their lives."

Think for a moment. Young people get plenty of exposure to the real world via television, newspapers, neighborhood children and adults, and community athletic programs. Besides, the first eighteen years hardly constitute a child's whole life.

Furthermore, Christian schools do not promise Utopia. Children are faced with many real life experiences within those hallowed halls. Students still misbehave, injustices still occur, and adults, students, and staff members will still have bad days and lose their tempers occasionally. Where there are humans, there will be imperfection. The difference between Christian schools and public schools, though, is that kids will see the problems dealt with from a Bible-centered perspective.

A more realistic objection for many parents is the cost factor. For most, the thought of paying tuition before college days is entirely out of the question, especially when they are already forking out substantial public school taxes.

But for those parents willing to make the sacrifice, I think a Christian elementary and/or secondary education is worth every penny. If before enrolling their children, Mom and Dad do their homework in exploring the doctrinal statements, educational philosophies, instructional practices, and teachers' educational backgrounds of the schools they are considering, their children's experiences are likely to be better. We should never be so trusting that we fail to ask questions of the administrators, teachers, staff members, students, and students' parents to see if what is stated in the public relations brochure is being put into practice.

If and when we decide to enroll our kids in a Christian school, we need to follow two basic guidelines. First, we need to be involved in our children's educations by checking homework, paying attention to notices from teachers and administrators, attending open houses and extracurricular activities, and volunteering our help if needed.

Second, we need to avoid the temptation to relegate our responsibility for making God real to our children to the school! It *is* a temptation: after all, the kids have Bible study and chapel every day, pray before classes, and spend most of their time with Christians.

Moms and Dads, we cannot rely on Christian schooling—or even the church, for that matter—to train up our children in the way they should go. Ultimately, the job of making God real to our children is *ours*.

Make Way for Grandmas and Grandpas!

Becoming a grandparent can sneak up on you before you know it. Take it from me—just *saying* the word for the very first time in reference to yourself can stick in your throat. *Have I really arrived at this point so soon?*

But we grandparents have unique roles to play in the lives of our grandchildren. Grandparents who choose to become more than casually involved in their grandchildren's growing-up years can really make a difference.

Writing to Timothy, a young man whose parents were of different faiths, the apostle Paul reminds him of the genuine faith his grandmother, Lois, and his mother, Eunice, passed on to him (2 Timothy 1:5). He urges Timothy to continue walking in the way he has known since childhood.

An inheritance like the one Grandma Lois bequeathed to Timothy doesn't just happen. It takes a deliberate decision by grandparents to be aware of and interested in their grandchildren's physical, emotional, mental, and spiritual welfare.

Today most grandparents find that life is full of opportunities, challenges, and commitments regardless of age. Some senior citizens may have time on their hands, but others claim they need to return to the work force to get some rest! Yet Christian grandparents may be vital links to helping their sons and daughters make God real to *their* children.

Wes's father, my children's Grandpa Chall, has been a powerful influence in our children's lives. I have already referred to those special one-on-one times he spent with Tom. Grandpa speaks up for his Lord—they are good friends, and he loves his Redeemer. It's always fun to talk with Grandpa about biblical issues and concerns; we come away having learned so much. When he prays right from the heart for the family he loves, we can feel God's presence in the room, and there is seldom a dry eye in the place.

In 1966 Grandpa gave his family a very special gift. It was a musical composition he had written just after the birth of our third child, Tom. Entitled, "Lullaby to My Grandchildren," it was included as one of the selections in a two-piano concert given at church by Grandpa Chall and our pastor's wife, Rosemary. We were so excited about it that, with the help of a friend in the jewelry business, we were able to present Grandpa with a music box featuring his lullaby. And the duplicate boxes we had made for each of our children are precious reminders of Grandpa's deep feelings for them.

My own eighty-year-old grandmother came to live with us when I was thirteen. We never played games together, nor did we shop or even bake cookies together. Grandma's health didn't allow her such luxuries. I can still see her head bowed in sleep as she sat in her beautifully carved oak rocker, her large Norwegian Bible open in her lap.

I knew without a doubt how much Jesus (she called Him *Yesus*) meant to Grandma. She told me so. I understood how much she wanted to be in heaven—she was ready to go "home." I remember visiting with her at times, but sleep claimed the major portion of her day. Her bathrobe became her everyday dress. Her wrinkled, gentle hands were no longer busy, as they had been in the days when she was raising her own nine children and acting as stepmother to five more. I remember my mother explaining to me that Grandma's spirit was young, but her body just wouldn't let her do what she wanted to.

In the years before her death, I never heard an angry or unkind word pass her lips. I remember wanting to be like her, to be as patient with others as she was with us. What an example she set, this woman who could have felt that her useful days were over!

If you are fortunate enough to have grandparents nearby who make time for your children, both generations will be richer for the experience. If your parents live far away or are no longer living, perhaps you could adopt an older couple, widow, or widower to include as a grandparent figure in your family's life.

Grandparents who live far away can still be included in their grandchildren's lives via letters, phone calls, and audio or videotape messages. Perhaps Grandma or Grandpa could record several children's stories, Bible stories, and prayers on tape. And when Johnny and Susie are older, they can read to their grandparents on cassettes! Those tapes, if preserved, will be even more precious when they are replayed years later—maybe for the great-grandchildren!

Grandparents can become involved in children's lives in many creative ways. Use your imagination, grandparents. Moms and dads, don't impose on your folks; they have their own agendas, too. But don't fail to take advantage of the profound influence their prayers and presence can have in making God real to your children.

Dear God, I'm All Alone

My mother raised three children alone. Oh, Dad was in our home, but as far as getting us to church on Sunday morning or teaching us about God's love for us, Mom was on her own. Sometimes Daddy came to church—I remember those days as wonderful occasions.

As a teenager I wished with all my heart that someone who was Christian would take a special interest in my dad; I was sure that then he would come to know Jesus as his Lord and Savior.

Dad always said, "If you have your health, you have everything." At the age of fifty-five he lost his health. During his lengthy illness, a Christian physician whom Dad had met on one of his infrequent visits to church became his friend. He was a man my dad respected, and he was able to lead my father to the Lord, all because he took the time to become involved in the life of a person with whom he had little in common.

That man's life influenced the lives of the three Leman children—and imagine what an example he was to his own kids, as well! We Lemans knew God was real to him as we witnessed his concern for the spiritual welfare of another human being.

Take a look around your sanctuary on Sunday morning. You will probably see many parents there who are alone in their faith, and some who are alone, period. It is tough raising children without a partner. Love and support from the family of God can make all the difference to parents who are single-handedly trying to make God real to their children.

A Parent's Prayer

Parenting is full of joys and sorrows, privileges and demands. For the Christian parent who wants to point his or her children to the living God, it's a real challenge! Somehow we view our children's decisions and actions in a more serious light because we consider them with eternal values in mind.

No book, no seminar, no counselor can guarantee that Christian parents will produce Christian children. It is not a matter of following steps one, two, three, and four—voila! Instant miniature Christians! God gave each of us freedom of choice, and it is up to each of our children to choose whether or not to follow God's ways.

Moreover, God in His graciousness and sovereignty can overrule our parenting mistakes and/or circumstances that have been beyond our control in the raising of our children. And He often does! Look at Moses, who lived in a godly home for only his first few years before he was claimed by the Egyptian Pharaoh's daughter, who had rescued him from certain death. But during those early childhood years his Hebrew mother nursed him, cuddled and loved him, and apparently told him of the one true God. Later in Moses' life those seeds of faith, planted early in his heart and mind, blossomed, and he became a leader of his people, worthy in the sight of God to receive His law and pass it on to the Israelites.

Roberta is a modern-day example of God's intervention in a child's life. As a preschooler she had attended church regularly with her family, but when she was about five her parents became bitterly disillusioned with the church. Roberta openly admits that as a teenager she didn't even know where the churches in her community were located.

But even though Roberta was a popular cheerleader and academic achiever in high school, she knew something was missing in her life. Her friends' drunken behavior at one of their final senior-year events prompted some soul-searching, which resulted in Roberta's asking God to take charge of her life. Roberta eventually decided to serve God as a professional church worker. Today her enthusiasm for the things of God and her love for people are a radiant testimony. I wish I knew what seeds of faith were planted in Roberta's life during those early preschool years to yield such abundant fruit in the life of this dynamic young woman!

Still, Christian parents cannot deny that God has made clear, in His Word, His ideal plan for raising children. The closer we try to adhere to the biblical principles and guide-lines discussed in this book, the more our children will be strengthened and encouraged to choose God's ways and to allow Him full control of their lives. Can we do less than to give them the best start possible?

The Bible records the prayer Jesus offered His disci-ples before He was crucified. It is a wise parent who also prays:

> Holy Father, keep them in your care—all those you have given me—so that they will be united just as we are, with none missing.
>
> John 17:11

When I stand with my entire family before our precious Jesus in the heavenly home He has prepared for all those who love Him, the words I long to hear are, "Well done, good and faithful servants. Come share a glorious eternity with Me."

Have you taken seriously your parental role in the spiritual growth and development of your children? Have you helped to make God real in their lives? It is a God-given mandate: "Show them who I AM."

Questions for Thought

1. My intentions are good, but am I in danger of allowing the demands of my housekeeping, job, church, or community to take precedence over my primary parental goal—making God real to my children?

2. How can I become effectively involved in my child's schooling so I'm aware of its impact on his or her spiritual growth?

3. Recognizing the valuable influences that aunts, uncles, cousins, and grandparents can have on my child's spiritual, mental, and emotional growth, what steps can I take to improve or allow more time for family interaction?

Appendix

—

Together Recipes for Parents and Kids

Here are some recipes, along with conversation and faith application possibilities, to use on "Fun Days and Sundays" with your children.

Homemade Applesauce

Your child can—
     wash apples.

Mom or Dad will—
     peel, cut apples into quarters, and core.

Your child can—
     cut the sections of apple with a plastic picnic knife, under Mom's or Dad's watchful eye, and place them in a saucepan. (Expect him or her to eat lots; that's part of the fun!) Allow your child to add a small amount of water, pouring out of a partly filled measuring cup.

Mom or Dad will—

place a cover on the pan and cook gently until apples are tender.

Your child can—

add sugar, a little at a time, until it tastes just right! Just be careful: The pan is hot! Cool. Then use a food mill or masher to reduce the pulp to desired consistency.

Conversation and Faith Application Possibilities.

- Where do apples come from?
- Who made apple trees?
- What other goodies can we make from apples? (This is a great time to introduce the story and songs from Walt Disney's "Johnny Appleseed." John Chapman, the original Johnny Appleseed, loved the Lord and considered his apple planting a way to bless others.)
- Also, be sure to look at the core, the seeds, and cut one around the equator so your child finds the star inside. And have him sniff that appley smell.
- Homemade applesauce makes a great gift for someone who needs a lift!

Dinnertime Chocolate Pudding

Your child can—

help you carefully open a box of instant chocolate pudding mix. Allow him or her to pour the appropriate amount of milk into the bowl and to add the chocolate powder. (Remember, have him pour out of containers that are only partly full.)

Young children love to use a hand-held rotary beater. Show your child first, though, how to hold it down in the bowl so as to minimize spatters. Once your child has finished beating the mixture (usually a few minutes longer than is required to produce a creamy pudding), assist him or her in spooning the mixture into dessert dishes. Chill as directed.

Want to Have Some More Fun?

Reserve a small amount of pudding to use for finger paint. Yes, finger paint! Invite your child to produce a masterpiece on a plastic tablecloth or Formica-topped surface. When he or she is tired of painting and tasting, you can reproduce the creation by simply covering it with a piece of construction paper. Press down, lift up and voila! You will have a priceless piece of chocolate art to adorn your refrigerator. It even smells good!

Conversation and Faith Application Possibilities.

- Where does chocolate come from?
- Who made the plants cocoa beans grow on?
- Does God love the people who harvest the beans?
- Why do you suppose God made food so much fun to taste and smell?

Gingerbread Children

Is there a cookie monster in your house? Kids love to help make cookies—especially gingerbread children. Here is an absolutely delicious version of the old favorite.

Ingredients:

1 cup vegetable shortening
1 cup white sugar

1 large egg
1 cup light molasses
2 tablespoons white vinegar stirred into 2 teaspoons
baking soda
½ teaspoon salt
5 cups all-purpose flour
2 teaspoons ginger
1 teaspoon cinnamon
1 teaspoon ground cloves

Your child can—

cream premeasured shortening and sugar with the back of a wooden spoon. (If you prefer to use an electric mixer, have your child add the ingredients. *You* run the mixer.)

Mom or Dad will—

crack the egg and place it in a measuring cup or bowl.

Your child can—

add the egg to the creamed mixture. He or she can also add other ingredients after you measure them and can continue to mix until the batter gets too stiff for little muscles to handle.

Mom or Dad will—

finish the mixing, then chill dough well. Roll out on lightly floured surface. Cut out and place gingerbread children on lightly greased cookie sheet. (Most children will prefer to have their own portions of dough to shape.) Bake at 375 degrees for four to five minutes. Do not overbake.

Your child can—

frost and decorate as desired, using ready-made or homemade frosting, a cake decorator, blunt knives, raisins (for buttons), and cinnamon imperials (for noses). Note: If time is a factor and you simply want a good cookie, roll the dough into balls and press lightly with a floured glass bottom. Bake as directed, cool, frost.

Conversation and Faith Application Possibilities.

- Tell the story of the gingerbread man who ran away from the kind old lady who made him.
- Talk about how God created us and how much He loves us. Do we sometimes run away from Him?
- Note the different personalities of each cookie person. We are all unique, too, with God-given gifts and abilities.

"The Best" Kids' Play Clay

2 cups unsifted flour
1 cup salt
4 teaspoons cream of tartar
2 cups water
2 tablespoons cooking oil
Several drops food coloring

Your child can—
combine the first three ingredients and, with some supervision, add the liquids.

Mom or Dad will—
cook over medium-high heat in saucepan, stirring constantly until mixture forms a ball. Turn onto a smooth surface and cool until comfortable to touch.

Your child can—

knead until smooth. Note: Store finished Play Clay in an airtight container. (It does not have to cool completely.) It will keep for a long time if stored properly. To clean saucepan, soak in cold water for several hours.

Conversation and Faith Application Possibilities.

Children love the consistency of this clay and will be entertained for long periods of time if you offer measuring cups, a rolling pin, plastic picnic knives, cookie cutters, and mini-muffin tins to assist them in playing "bakery," "store," "factory," etc. A vinyl cloth will protect the tabletop. A pair of children's safety scissors will provide tons of fun as little ones cut the clay into tiny pieces, then gather it up again. (They may need your help!) What a natural way to increase preschoolers' cutting skills.

As they play, talk about:

- the creation story
- Isaiah 64:8; Jeremiah 18:6; Romans 9:21, which tell how God works to shape us into people who are more like Him
- making some Play Clay for a sick friend or for an upcoming birthday or Christmas gift